JUNIOR Picture Dictionary

JUNIOR
Picture
Dictionary

Miles Kelly

First published in 2011 by Miles Kelly Publishing Ltd
Harding's Barn, Bardfield End Green, Thaxted, Essex, CM6 3PX, UK

Copyright © Miles Kelly Publishing Ltd 2011

This edition printed 2019

6 8 10 9 7

Publishing Director Belinda Gallagher
Creative Director Jo Cowan
Editors Fran Bromage, Claire Philip, Sarah Parkin
Editorial Assistant Lauren White
Designers Joe Jones, Kayleigh Allen
Cover illustrator Dan Rieley
Image Manager Liberty Newton
Production Elizabeth Collins, Jennifer Brunwin-Jones
Reprographics Stephan Davis, Jennifer Hunt, Callum Ratcliffe-Bingham
Assets Lorraine King

ISBN 978-1-78617-859-6

Printed in China

British Library Cataloguing-in-Publication Data
A catalogue record for this book is available from the British Library

ACKNOWLEDGEMENTS
All artwork from the Miles Kelly Artwork Bank

The publishers would like to thank NASA for the use of their photograph on page 29

Made with paper from a sustainable forest

www.mileskelly.net

CONTENTS

UNIVERSE 14 — 53

PLANET EARTH 54–97

PREHISTORIC LIFE 98–131

PLANTS 132-167

ANIMALS 168–321

HUMAN BODY 322–353

TRANSPORT 354–375

UNIVERSE

Astronaut
Special spacesuits allow astronauts to leave their spacecraft and explore outer space

The Big Bang

The vast explosion that caused the beginning of the Universe

1 At the beginning of the Universe, a huge explosion blasted out vast amounts of energy

2 Millions of years later, gases clustered into clouds

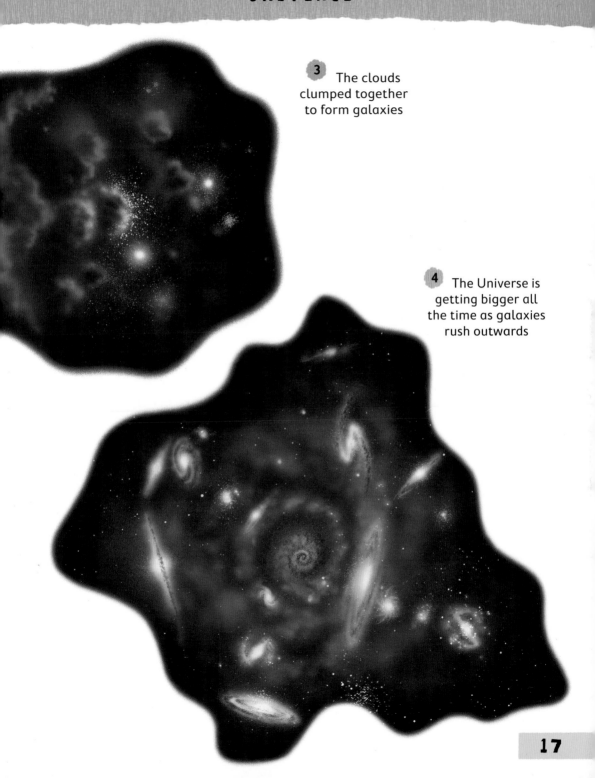

3 The clouds clumped together to form galaxies

4 The Universe is getting bigger all the time as galaxies rush outwards

17

Life of a star

Stars are different sizes depending
on how old they are — they live
for millions of years

(2) Gas and dust spin
together, growing
hotter and hotter until a
new star starts to shine

(1) Gas and dust
collect in a big
cloud called a
nebula

(3) Once the gas
and dust have
blown away, the
star can be seen

4 Towards the end of its life, a star may become a red giant

Galaxies

Giant groups of stars are called galaxies,
and there are different types in the Universe

Spiral
Barred spiral
Elliptical

Dense core   Spiralling
arms

Two arms
linked by a bar

Irregular
Two galaxies colliding

Tails of
stars being
pulled out

The Milky Way

There are billions of stars, including
the Sun, in our spiral galaxy

At the middle are
clouds of dust and gas

The 'arms' at the edge
contain lots of young,
bright stars

Side view

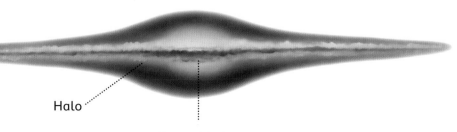

Halo

Central bulge

The Solar System

Our Solar System includes the Sun and all
of the planets travelling around it

Orbiting planets

The planets orbit (travel around) the
Sun. Each moves at a different speed

Mars

Venus

Earth

Mercury

Jupiter

Sun

Neptune

Uranus

Saturn

Pluto
Dwarf planet

The Sun

Sunspot
Cooler patches show
up as dark spots

Solar flare
Hot gases shoot up
from the surface

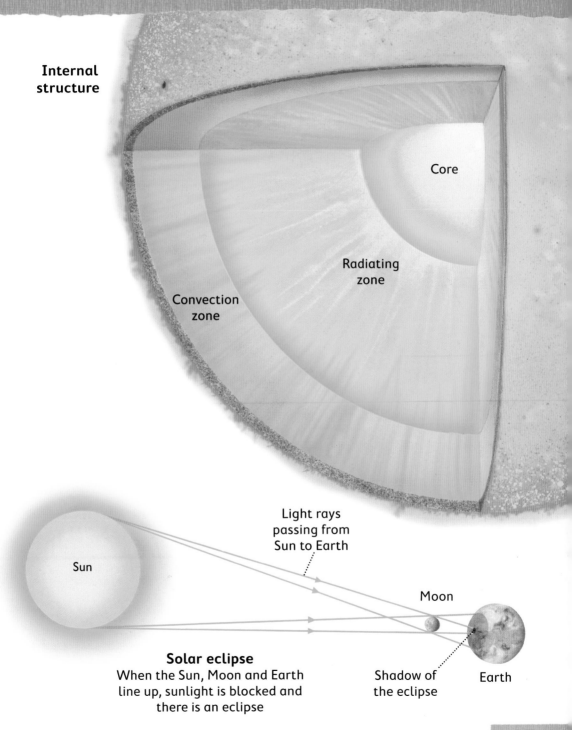

Internal structure

Core

Radiating zone

Convection zone

Light rays passing from Sun to Earth

Sun

Moon

Solar eclipse
When the Sun, Moon and Earth line up, sunlight is blocked and there is an eclipse

Shadow of the eclipse

Earth

Mercury

Position from Sun

Surface

Space rocks
hit the surface
leaving craters

Sun rising

Venus

Position from Sun

Venus has hundreds of volcanoes under its clouds

Surface

Earth

Position from Sun

Formation

1 Cloud starts to spin

2 Dust gathers into balls of rock, which form a small planet

3 The Earth begins to cool and a hard shell forms

4 Volcanoes erupt, releasing gases, which help to form the first atmosphere

5 The Earth was made up of one large piece of land, but is now split into seven continents

28

Mars

Position from Sun

Valles Marineris –
Mars' enormous
valley

Olympus Mons –
the largest volcano
in the Solar System

Surface

Dry, desert-like surface
covered in red dust

Jupiter

Jupiter's fast winds blow clouds into coloured bands

Position from Sun

300-year-old storm,
The Great Red Spot

Galilean moons
Jupiter's four biggest moons

Ganymede

Callisto

Io

Europa

Surface of Jupiter

Great Red Spot

Io

Saturn

Position from Sun

Rings

Chunks
of ice

Uranus

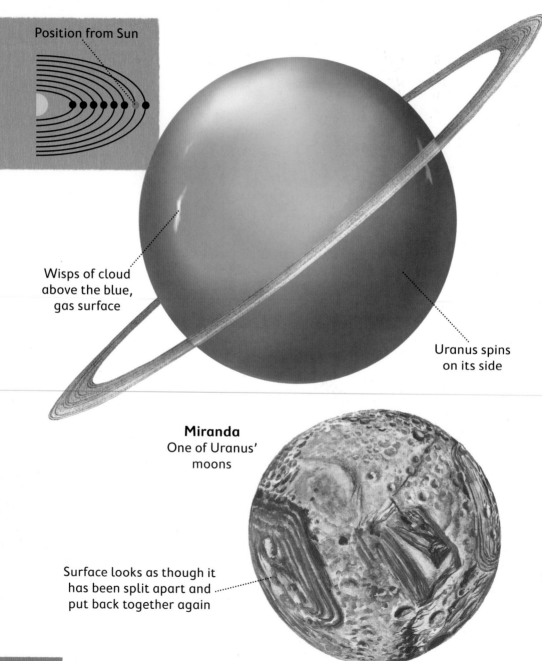

Position from Sun

Wisps of cloud
above the blue,
gas surface

Uranus spins
on its side

Miranda
One of Uranus'
moons

Surface looks as though it
has been split apart and
put back together again

Neptune

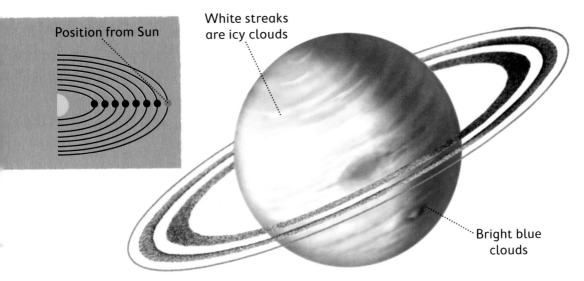

Position from Sun

White streaks
are icy clouds

Bright blue
clouds

Neptune

Surface of Triton
One of Neptune's moons

The Moon

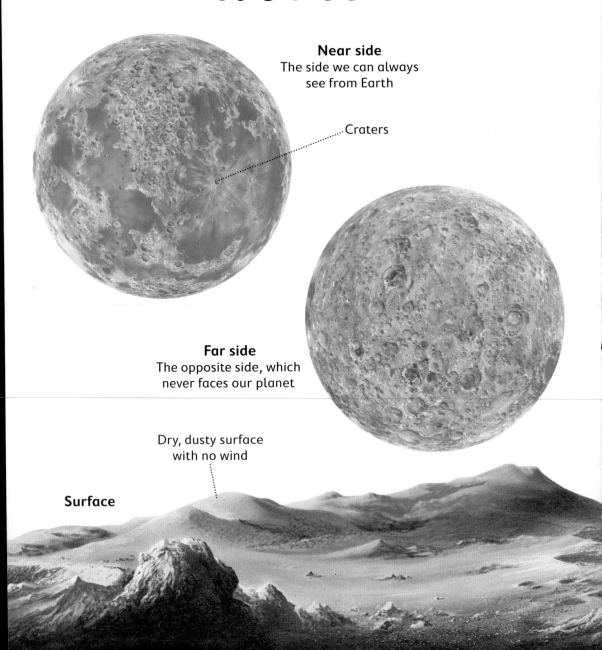

Near side
The side we can always
see from Earth

Craters

Far side
The opposite side, which
never faces our planet

Dry, dusty surface
with no wind

Surface

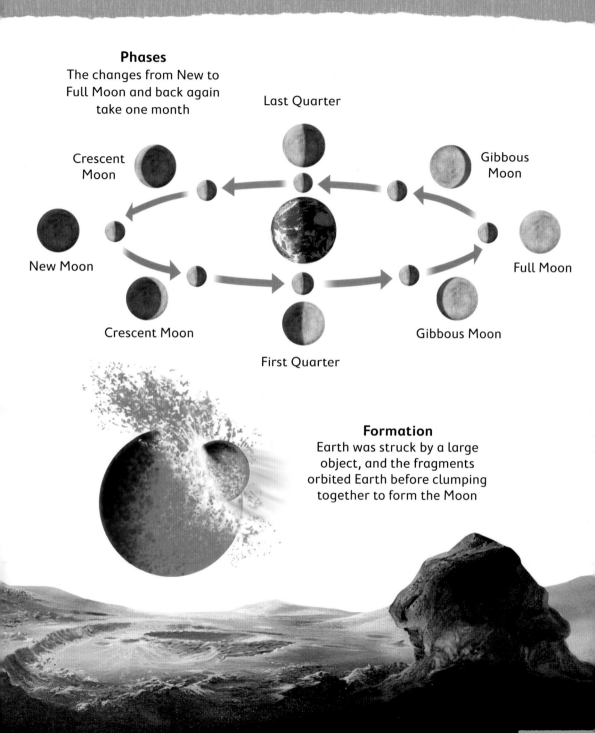

Phases

The changes from New to Full Moon and back again take one month

Last Quarter

Crescent Moon

Gibbous Moon

New Moon

Full Moon

Crescent Moon

Gibbous Moon

First Quarter

Formation

Earth was struck by a large object, and the fragments orbited Earth before clumping together to form the Moon

Comets, asteroids and meteors

Inside a comet

Jets of gas

Nucleus

Solid core of rock

Dust and ice surrounds core

Coma

Comet
Bright objects with long tails, which streak across the night sky

Gas tail

Halley's Comet
This comet passes Earth roughly every 75 years and is shown here on the Bayeux Tapestry with the Battle of Hastings in 1066

Jupiter

Mars

Asteroids
Large chunks
of rock

Most asteroids circle
the Sun between
Mars and Jupiter in
the Asteroid Belt

Dust tail

Meteors
Small space rocks

Telescopes and observatories

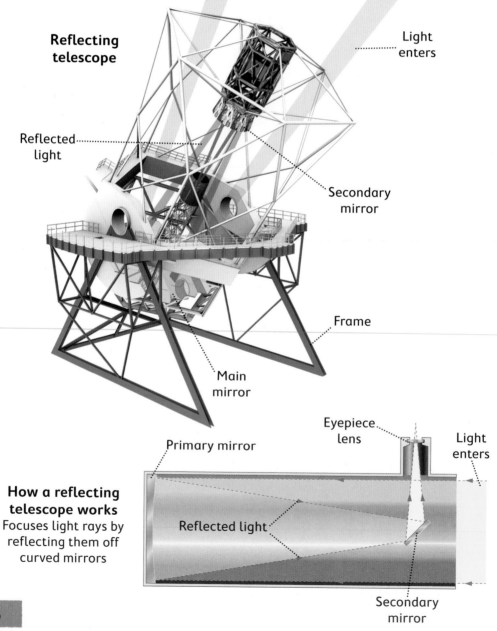

Reflecting telescope

Light enters

Reflected light

Secondary mirror

Frame

Main mirror

Primary mirror

Eyepiece lens

Light enters

How a reflecting telescope works
Focuses light rays by reflecting them off curved mirrors

Reflected light

Secondary mirror

Early telescopes

Hershel's telescope (1789)

Newton's telescope (1668)

Observatory
Equipped with instruments such as telescopes to study the night sky

Rotating dome

Raised shutter

Telescope inside

Building linking telescopes

Star charts

Different constellations (star patterns) can
be seen depending on your position on the planet

Ophiuchus
(*Serpent Bearer*)

Aquila
(*Eagle*)

Hercules
(*Strongman*)

Serpens
(*Serpent*)

Lyra
(*Lyre*)

Sagitta
(*Arrow*)

Equuleus
(*Foal*)

Corona Borealis
(*Northern Crown*)

Delphinus
(*Dolphin*)

Boötes
(*Herdsman*)

Cygnus
(*Swan*)

Draco
(*Dragon*)

Pegasus
(*Winged Horse*)

Coma Berenices
(*Berenice's Hair*)

Lacerta
(*Lizard*)

Virgo
(*Virgin*)

Canes Venatici
(*Hunting Dogs*)

Cepheus
(*King*)

Andromeda
(*Chained
Princess*)

Leo
(*Lion*)

Ursa Minor
(*Little Bear*)

Pisces
(*Fishes*)

Ursa Major
(*Great Bear*)

Cassiopeia
(*Queen*)

Camelopardalis
(*Giraffe*)

Triangulum
(*Triangle*)

Leo Minor
(*Little Lion*)

Lynx (*Lynx*)

Perseus
(*Hero*)

Aries
(*Ram*)

Cancer
(*Crab*)

Hydra
(*Sea Serpent*)

Auriga
(*Charioteer*)

Cetus
(*Whale*)

Gemini
(*Twins*)

Taurus (*Bull*)

Orion
(*Hunter*)

Canis Minor
(*Little Dog*)

Constellations visible from
the Northern Hemisphere
The half of the Earth that is
north of the Equator

Constellations visible from the Southern Hemisphere
The half of the Earth that is south of the Equator

Lepus (*Hare*)

Canis Major (*Great Dog*)

Columba (*Dove*)

Eridanus (*River Eridanus*)

Puppis (*Stern*), Carina (*Keel*) and Vela (*Sail*)

Caelum (*Chisel*)

Pictor (*Painter's Easel*)

Fornax (*Furnace*)

Sextans (*Sextant*)

Hydra (*Sea Serpent*)

Recticulum (*Net*)

Dorado (*Goldfish*)

Phoenix (*Phoenix*)

Cetus (*Whale*)

Volans (*Flying Fish*)

Crater (*Cup*)

Crux (*Southern Cross*)

Chamaeleon (*Chameleon*)

Grus (*Crane*), Tucana (*Toucan*), and Pavo (*Peacock*)

Musca (*Fly*)

Apus (*Bird of Paradise*)

Centaurus (*Centaur*)

Corvus (*Crow*)

Triangulum Australe (*Southern Triangle*)

Indus (*Indian*)

Aquarius (*Water Carrier*)

Virgo (*Virgin*)

Ara (*Altar*)

Corona Australis (*Southern Crown*)

Piscis Austrinus (*Southern Fish*)

Scorpius (*Scorpion*)

Capricornus (*Sea Goat*)

Libra (*Scales*)

Serpens (*Serpent*) and Ophiuchus (*Serpent Bearer*)

Sagittarius (*Archer*)

Constellations

Some star patterns can be seen
from both the Northern and
Southern hemispheres

Aquila
Eagle

Delphinus
Dolphin

Orion
Hunter

Canis Minor
Little Dog

Serpens
Serpent

Pegasus
Winged Horse

Equuleus
Little Horse

Lepus
Hare

Corona Borealis
Northern Crown

Vulpecula
Fox

Monoceros
Unicorn

Corvus
Crow

Probes

Unmanned, computer-controlled spacecraft

Voyager 1

Voyager 2

Venus Express

Cassini-Huygens

Galileo

Mariner 9

Radio aerial

Solar panel

Camera

Artificial satellites

Spacecraft that orbit the Earth

Communications satellite

Weather satellite

Explorer 1
Exploratory satellite

Sputnik 1
First satellite in space

Antenna

Hubble Space Telescope
Orbits Earth to take photos of the Universe

Solar panel

Exploring the Moon

Saturn V
The rocket that launched the Apollo spacecraft, which touched down on the Moon in 1969

Launch escape tower

Service module

Third stage

Command module

Second stage

Lunar module

J-2 engines

J-2 engine

First stage

Moon

Apollo spacecraft returns to Earth

F-1 engines

Earth

Third stage of Saturn V detaches from Apollo spacecraft

Key

Journey to the Moon
Journey back to Earth

Saturn V journey
The craft circled Earth first before speeding towards the Moon

Apollo spacecraft

Command and service module

Lunar module

Key
1 Landing pad
2 Hatch
3 Antenna
4 Thruster
5 Rocket

Lunar module landing
The lander detached from
the main craft to touch
down on the surface

Space shuttle

Spacelab, a laboratory where crew can carry out experiments

Crew quarters where astronauts eat, sleep and work

Access tunnel from crew cabin to Spacelab

Flight deck with pilot's control

Antonov AN-225
The biggest, heaviest plane in the world can transport space shuttles

Space shuttle

Shuttle flight

This shuttle is being used to place a satellite in space

4 Shuttle goes into orbit around the Earth

3 Main fuel tank falls away 130 kilometres up

5 Shuttle crew place satellite in space

6 Shuttle positions itself to re-enter the Earth's atmosphere

7 Shuttle lands like a glider

2 Solid-fuel rocket burners fall away 45 kilometres up

1 Shuttle blasts off using its own engines and two solid rocket boosters

8 Landing

Space stations

International Space Station (ISS)
The latest and largest space station will
look like this when complete

Close-up of the ISS
The space shuttle delivers supplies
such as food and equipment

Skylab
The first US
space station

Key

1 Solar panels for power

2 Docking port

3 Space shuttle

4 Control module

5 Living module

6 Soyuz ferry

Spacesuit

An astronaut's spacesuit includes
clothing and equipment

Camera

Manned Manoeuvring
Unit (jet pack)

Joystick
control

Visor

Glove

Sleeping bag
Astronauts sleep
in sleeping bags
attached to walls

Long tube fastens
astronaut to the
spacecraft

Astronaut
Special suits allow
astronauts to work
outside their spacecraft

PLANET EARTH

Volcano
When a volcano erupts,
magma (molten rock
below the Earth's surface)
is expelled

Earth

Earth's chemistry

Element	Percentage
Iron	35.0
Oxygen	28.0
Magnesium	17.0
Silicon	13.0
Nickel	2.7
Sulphur	2.7
Calcium	0.6
Other	0.6
Aluminium	0.4

Internal structure

Crust

Mantle

Outer core

Inner core

ASIA

NORTH AMERICA

EUROPE

AFRICA

SOUTH AMERICA

OCEANIA

Continents
The Earth is split into seven main divisions of land

ANTARCTICA

Spinning Earth

Our planet spins constantly as it orbits the Sun

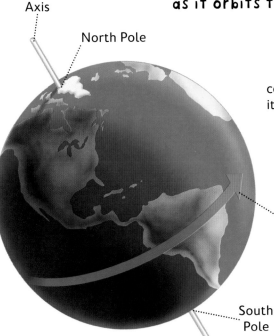

Axis

North Pole

Direction of spin

South Pole

Axis
In one day, the Earth completes one full rotation on its axis, a tilted imaginary line which joins the North and South Poles

Magnetic poles

At the centre of the Earth is liquid iron. As the Earth spins, it makes the iron behave like a magnet

Lines show direction of magnetic force

Orbiting the Sun
It takes 365 days (one year) for the Earth to travel around the Sun

Continental drift

The slow movement of Earth's continents over millions of years

Key

1. Pacific plate
2. North American plate
3. South American plate
4. African plate
5. Eurasian plate
6. Indian-Australian plate
7. Antarctic plate

Tectonic plates
Earth's surface is broken into sections that are always shifting. The seven largest are shown here

Drifting continents
Over millions of years, Earth's land has moved and changed to form the seven continents we live on today

1 **220 million years ago (mya)**

PANGEA

PANTHALASSA OCEAN

TETHYS SEA

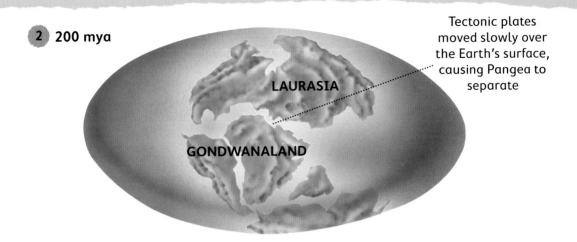

2 **200 mya**

LAURASIA

GONDWANALAND

Tectonic plates moved slowly over the Earth's surface, causing Pangea to separate

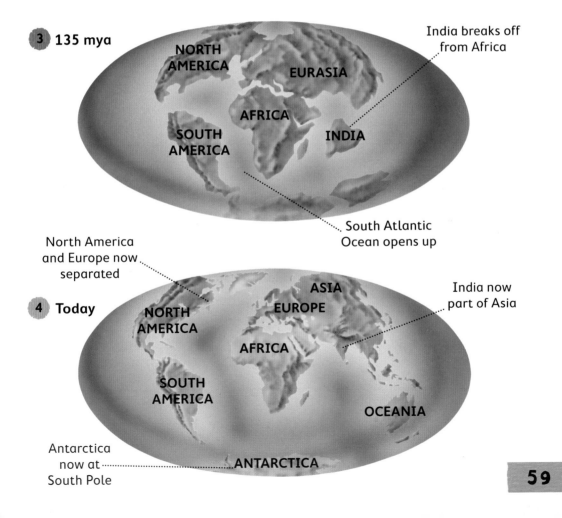

3 **135 mya**

NORTH AMERICA

EURASIA

AFRICA

SOUTH AMERICA

INDIA

India breaks off from Africa

South Atlantic Ocean opens up

North America and Europe now separated

4 **Today**

NORTH AMERICA

ASIA
EUROPE

AFRICA

SOUTH AMERICA

OCEANIA

ANTARCTICA

India now part of Asia

Antarctica now at South Pole

Rock cycle

Rocks form deep inside the Earth, move and
sometimes change. They go up to the surface
and eventually return below the ground

Erosion and
transport

Weathering at
the surface

Laying down
sediment

Sedimentary rock

Burial becoming
more compact
under pressure

Deep burial and
metamorphism
(changing structure)

Magma forms
crystals as it cools

Igneous rock

Metamorphic rock

Melting to
magma

61

Erosion

Many different forces can break down rock

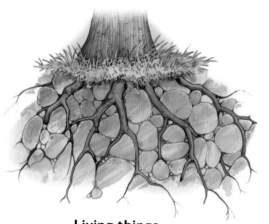

Living things
The roots of trees can crack
open rock as they grow

Temperature
When a rock warms up and cools
down, it changes in size and weakens
– sometimes large flakes break off

Wind
Sand-carrying wind carves
away parts of rock

Smooth
rock face

Arch

PLANET EARTH

Waterfall
Where a river flows from hard rock to soft rock, the softer rock is worn away faster

Cirque

Hard rock overhang

Crevasses (cracks)

Basin

Fallen rocks

Plunge pool

Moraine (debris)

Movement of glacier

Soft rock gets worn away

Meltwater

Snout

Glacier
Huge areas of ice form near mountaintops then slide down eroding rocks as they melt

Cliff undercut by crashing waves

Cliff

Waves

Sand

Wave
Winds whip up waves that wear down rocky cliffs as they hit the surface

Rocks from fallen cliff

Pebbles

Rocks

Combinations of particles from one or more minerals

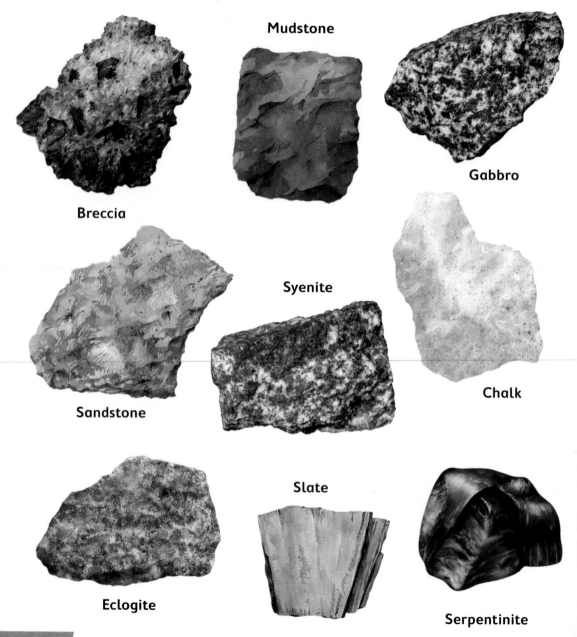

Breccia

Mudstone

Gabbro

Sandstone

Syenite

Chalk

Eclogite

Slate

Serpentinite

Minerals

The natural chemicals from which rocks are made

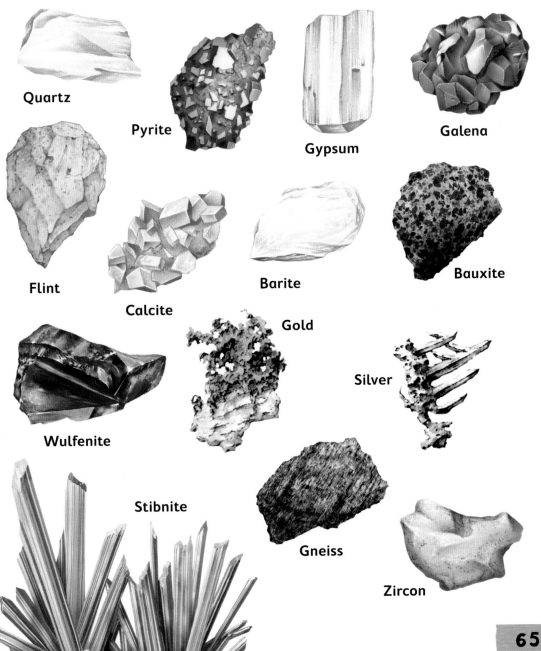

Quartz

Pyrite

Gypsum

Galena

Flint

Calcite

Barite

Bauxite

Gold

Wulfenite

Silver

Stibnite

Gneiss

Zircon

Gemstones

Crystals of natural minerals that are often used in jewellery. Everybody has a birthstone, depending on which month they were born in

Garnet
January

Amethyst
February

Aquamarine
March

Diamond
April

Emerald
May

Pearl
June

Ruby
July

Peridot
August

Sapphire
September

Opal
October

Topaz
November

Turquoise
December

Amber
Not all gems are stone – tree sap hardens to form amber

Imperial State Crown
One of the British Crown Jewels

Diamond

Fossils such as this fly are often found stuck in amber

Pearl

Ruby

Sapphire

Emerald

Volcanoes

Places where magma (red-hot liquid rock)
emerges through the Earth's crust
and onto the surface

Internal view

Key

1 Main vent

2 Clouds of ash, steam and smoke

3 Lava flowing away from vent

4 Branch pipe

5 Magma chamber

6 Layers of rock from previous eruptions

Volcano types

Shield volcano
This has a low, wide shape
with gently sloping sides

Crater volcano
Made when the top
of a cone-shaped
volcano explodes
and sinks into the
magma chamber

Cone-shaped volcano
This has steep sides built up
of layers of lava and ash

68

Lava bombs
Flying lumps of lava are given names depending on their shape

Pele's tears

Ribbon bomb

Cowpat bomb

Types of lava
Liquid rock ejected from a volcano

Spindle bomb

Aa lava
Slow-flowing lava has a jagged surface

Breadcrust bomb

Pahoehoe lava
Fast-flowing lava cools to form smooth, rope-like rock

Earthquakes

Sudden trembles caused by the movement of the Earth's crust

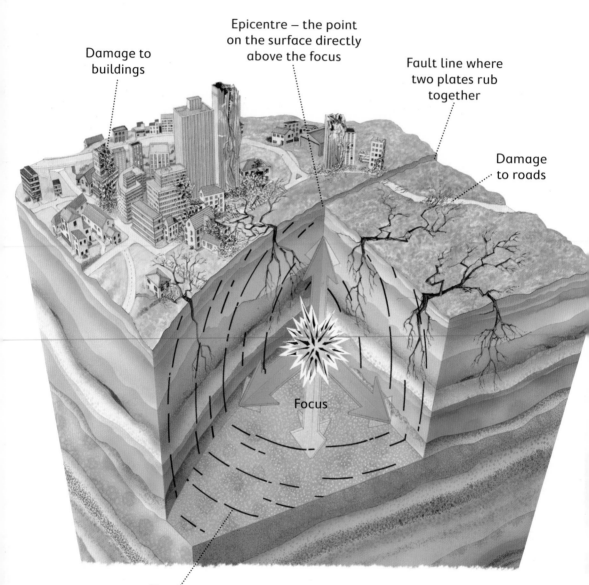

Damage to buildings

Epicentre – the point on the surface directly above the focus

Fault line where two plates rub together

Damage to roads

Focus

Shock waves from the focus

Tsunamis

Enormous waves produced by an earthquake or volcanic eruption under the sea

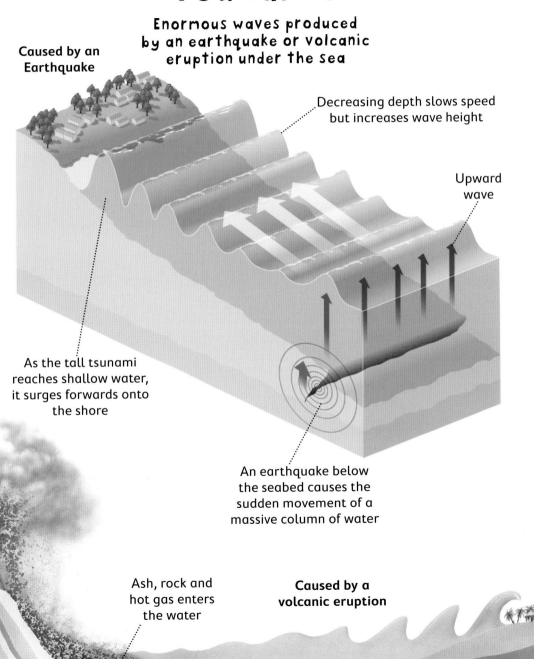

Caused by an Earthquake

Decreasing depth slows speed but increases wave height

Upward wave

As the tall tsunami reaches shallow water, it surges forwards onto the shore

An earthquake below the seabed causes the sudden movement of a massive column of water

Ash, rock and hot gas enters the water

Caused by a volcanic eruption

71

Mountains

Formation
These diagrams show three
different ways mountains can form

Fold mountain

Mountain range
is pushed up

Folded and
uplifted rock

Himalayas
The mountains in
this range in Asia
are fold mountains

Folded rock
layers

Asian
plate

Direction of Indian
plate movement

Indian plate

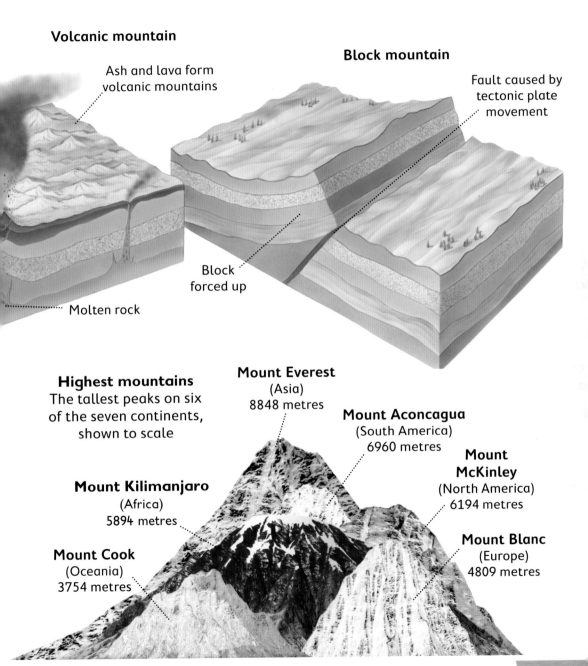

Volcanic mountain

Ash and lava form volcanic mountains

Block mountain

Fault caused by tectonic plate movement

Block forced up

Molten rock

Highest mountains
The tallest peaks on six of the seven continents, shown to scale

Mount Everest
(Asia)
8848 metres

Mount Aconcagua
(South America)
6960 metres

Mount McKinley
(North America)
6194 metres

Mount Kilimanjaro
(Africa)
5894 metres

Mount Blanc
(Europe)
4809 metres

Mount Cook
(Oceania)
3754 metres

Oceans

ARCTIC OCEAN

ATLANTIC
OCEAN

PACIFIC
OCEAN

PACIFIC
OCEAN

INDIAN
OCEAN

SOUTHERN OCEAN

High tide
The sea moves
upwards and inland
as the tide rises

Low tide
The sea ebbs,
retreating as the
tide drops

74

Ocean currents

In the ocean, water is continually moving, passing around the globe in giant streams called currents

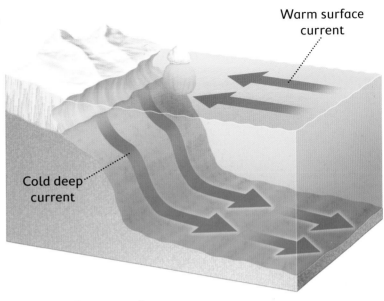

Warm surface current

Cold deep current

Ocean floor

Continental slope

Land

Continental shelf

Sea mount

Spreading ridge

Abyssal trench

Abyssal hills

Ocean trench

Volcanic island

Island formation

Volcanic island formation

1 Volcano erupting on the seabed – molten rock breaks through the Earth's crust

2 As more lava is deposited on the seabed, a cone shape builds up

3 The lava breaks the water's surface, forming a new island

Atoll (coral island) formation

1 When coral grows around an island's coasts, first a fringing reef develops

2 The island drops, or the sea rises, and the coral becomes a barrier reef

3 When there is no longer any sign of the island, the reef is called an atoll

Cave formation

1 Water seeps through cracks in rock

2 Underground stream carves into rock

3 Large cave system develops

Cave features

Key

1 Waterfall in sink hole

2 Shaft

3 Waterfall

4 Gallery

5 Cave opening

Rock pool

As the tide retreats, pools of water are
trapped on rocky beaches creating homes
for many seashore species

Key

1 Anemone
2 Limpet
3 Blenny fish
4 Prawn
5 Velvet crab
6 Starfish
7 Hermit crab
8 Sea urchin
9 Shore crab
10 Top shell
11 Razor shell
12 Mussel

Rivers

River course

In its upper reaches, a river tumbles over rocks through steep valleys

In its middle reaches, a river winds through broad valleys

Oxbow lake

Meander

In its lower reaches, a river winds broadly and smoothly across flat floodplains

Over flat land, a river may split into branches

Mud and sand deposits build up land

Outlets

Delta
Rivers slow down as they flow into the sea and often dump mud and sand in a fan-shape, or delta

River

Lakes

Formation

Landslide across a river

Blocked water forms a lake

The Great Lakes
The largest group of freshwater lakes on the border of the United States and Canada

Lake Superior

Lake Huron

Lake Michigan

Lake Erie

Lake Ontario

Crater Lake
The deepest lake in the United States is in Oregon. It has a small volcano called Wizard Island in the middle

Seashore

A place where the sea meets the land

Key

1 Shingle beach
2 Shingle spit
3 Stump
4 Needle
5 Stack
6 Arch
7 Headland
8 Cave
9 Circular bay
10 Waves
11 Cliffs
12 River
13 Delta
14 Mudflats
15 Saltmarsh
16 Sandy beach

Rainforests

Emergent tree

Main canopy

Understorey

Shrubs

Deforestation
Forests are being destroyed
to clear the land for
farming and housing

Natural forest

Trees are burnt

Farm crops

Rain washes away topsoil

Soil becomes useless

Deserts

Barchan dune

Oasis

Ridges of sand being
blown into dunes

Rock beneath
the desert

Sand dunes
Depending on the type of
wind and sand, dunes form in
different shapes and patterns

Transverse dune

Seif dune

Barchan dune

Parabolic dune

Star dune

85

Atmosphere

Layers of gases surround Earth in a 'blanket'

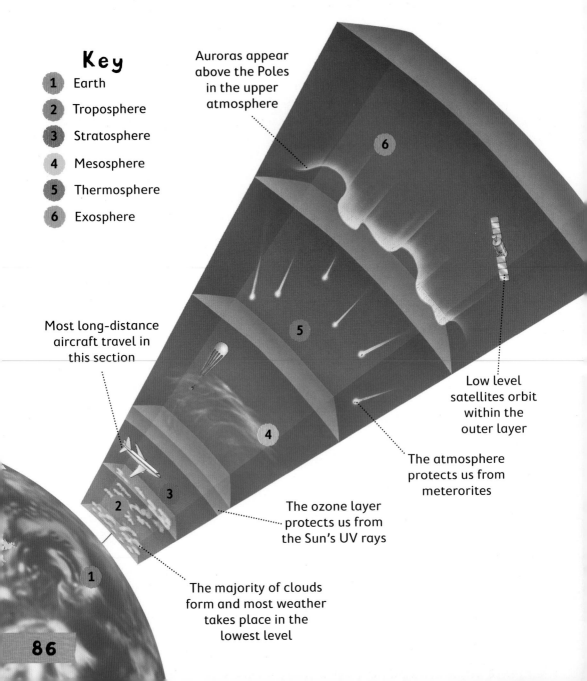

Key

1 Earth

2 Troposphere

3 Stratosphere

4 Mesosphere

5 Thermosphere

6 Exosphere

Auroras appear above the Poles in the upper atmosphere

Most long-distance aircraft travel in this section

Low level satellites orbit within the outer layer

The atmosphere protects us from meterorites

The ozone layer protects us from the Sun's UV rays

The majority of clouds form and most weather takes place in the lowest level

Global warning

Too much carbon dioxide, which can be caused by pollution, in the atmosphere causes Earth's temperature to rise

Some heat
bounces back

Sun

Carbon dioxide
layer traps heat

Heat from
the Sun

Trapped heat
bounces back
to Earth

87

Water cycle

On Earth, water is continually
rising and falling in a cycle

Key

1 Water evaporates from
the sea

2 Water vapour condenses
to form clouds

3 Clouds rise

4 Water vapour is given off
by forests

5 Clouds become larger and
heavier as more water
vapour sticks together

6 Clouds become too heavy —
the water falls to land
as rain

7 Rain falls into rivers, which
run back to the sea

88

Clouds

Billions of water droplets form clouds in the sky. There are many different shapes and sizes

1

6

7

4

2

8

5

3

Key

1 Virga

2 Cumulonimbus

3 Cumulus

4 Cirrostratus

5 Stratus

6 Cirrus

7 Contrails

8 Stratocumulus

Formation

Clouds form when warm, rising air meets lower temperatures, such as at mountaintops

Thundercloud
In a thunderstorm, a negative charge from the cloud meets a positive charge from the ground to create lightning

Positive charge

Negative charge

Lightning – a giant spark of electricity

Positive charge

Hailstone formation

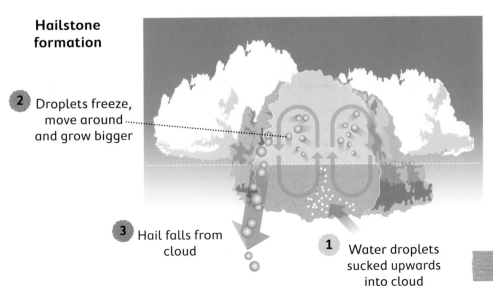

2 Droplets freeze, move around and grow bigger

3 Hail falls from cloud

1 Water droplets sucked upwards into cloud

91

Wind

The world's main wind patterns

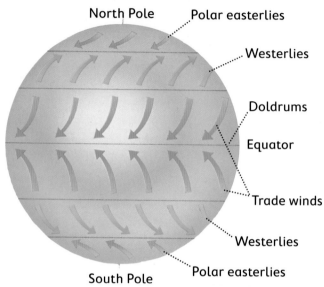

North Pole

Polar easterlies

Westerlies

Doldrums

Equator

Trade winds

Westerlies

Polar easterlies

South Pole

Beaufort Scale
The numbered scale that measures wind force

0: Calm

1: Light air

2: Light breeze

3: Gentle breeze

4: Moderate breeze

5: Fresh breeze

6: Strong breeze

7: Near gale

8: Gale

9: Strong gale

10: Storm

11: Violent storm

12: Hurricane

Tornado
Formed when thunderclouds start spinning. The spinning air forms a funnel that reaches down to the ground

Hurricane
Tropical storms start at sea when strong winds blow into an area of low pressure and start spinning very fast

Storm whirls around a central 'eye'

Weather map

These charts use symbols to show the constantly changing weather conditions

Key

Warm front: warm air rises over cold air giving rain

Cold front: cold air pushes warm air upwards giving heavy showers

Occluded front: a cold front meets a warm front

Isobars: connect places with the same air pressure

Line: wind strength
Circle: cloud cover

Strong wind (three lines on tail)

Area of calm with lots of cloud cover

Climate

The weather conditions of a specific area or region

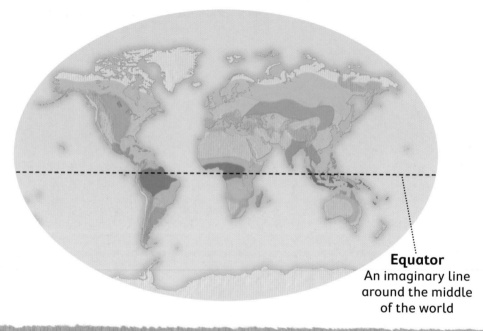

Equator
An imaginary line
around the middle
of the world

Key

Around the world there are different climates.
The warmest are found close to the Equator

Tropical forest

Tropical grassland

Mountainous

Dry temperate

Wet temperate

Desert

Polar

Temperate grassland

Cold temperate

Cycle of seasons

As the Earth spins on a tilt, different parts of its
surface face the Sun — giving us yearly seasons

**Seasons in the
Northern Hemisphere**

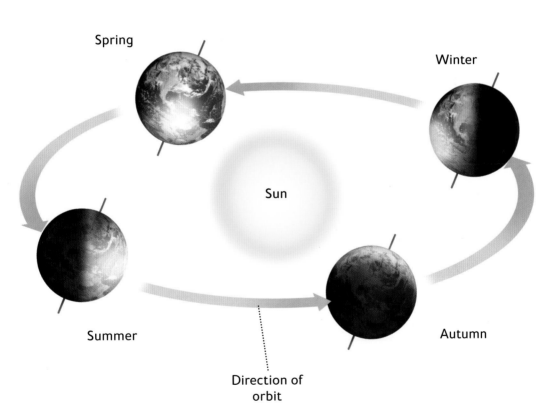

Spring

Winter

Sun

Summer

Autumn

Direction of
orbit

Pteranodon
This huge flying reptile lived
long before birds, about
70 million years ago in the
Late Cretaceous Period

PREHISTORIC LIFE

Elasmosaurus
Prehistoric monsters
such as this long-necked
marine reptile once
inhabited the Earth

Fossil formation

Fossils are the remains of animals and
plants that died a very long time ago
and became preserved in rocks

Living ichthyosaur –
a prehistoric reptile

1 After death, the
ichthyosaur sinks to the
seabed. Worms, crabs
and other scavengers eat
its soft body parts

3 Millions of years later
the upper rock layers wear
away and the fossil
remains are exposed

2 Sediments cover
the hard body parts,
such as bones and
teeth, which
gradually turn into
solid rock

PREHISTORIC LIFE

Fossil timeline
Scientists who study rocks (geologists) can work out how old a rock is by studying the fossils within it

Diatryma

Neanderthal

Lambeosaur

Deinotherium

Archaeopteryx

Acanthodes

Hoplopteryx

Allosaurus

Thrinaxodon

Dimetrodon

Ammonite

Amphibian

Dragonfly

Shark tooth

Trilobite

NEOGENE
24 million years ago (mya) onwards

PALAEOGENE
65–24 mya

CRETACEOUS
144–65 mya

JURASSIC
203–144 mya

PERMIAN-TRIASSIC
295–203 mya

DEVONIAN-CARBONIFEROUS
410–295 mya

CAMBRIAN-ORDOVICIAN
540–435 mya

Plants

Cooksonia

Archaefructus

Flowers

Jurassic landscape

Cycad

Archaeopteryx

Cycad

Monkey
puzzle tree

Gingko leaf

Lichen

Magnolia
flower

Tree fern

Sea life

Ammonite
Early shellfish

Crinoids
Simple marine animals —
these examples are dying

Charnia
Early type of coral

Jellyfish

Ottoia
Early sea worm

Feather-like body
to catch food

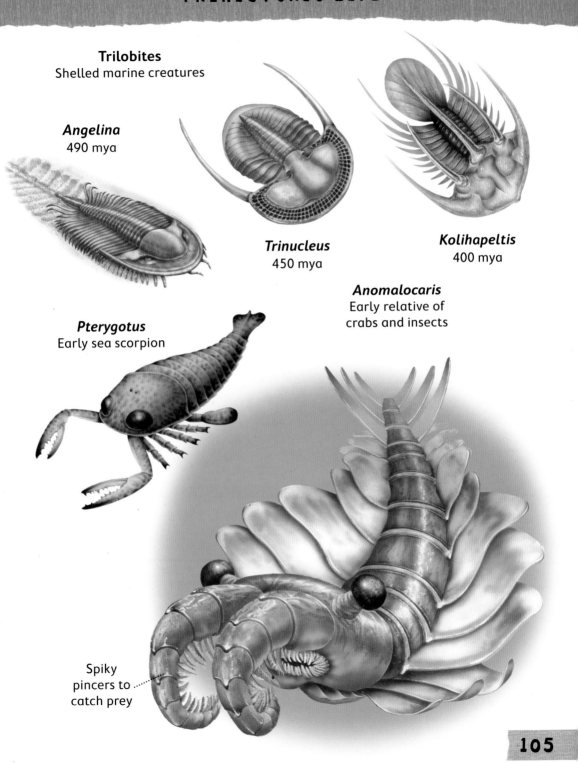

Trilobites
Shelled marine creatures

Angelina
490 mya

Trinucleus
450 mya

Kolihapeltis
400 mya

Anomalocaris
Early relative of
crabs and insects

Pterygotus
Early sea scorpion

Spiky
pincers to ......
catch prey

Fish

Pikaia

Tail fin

Cephalaspis

Climatius

Dunkleosteus
An armoured fish

106

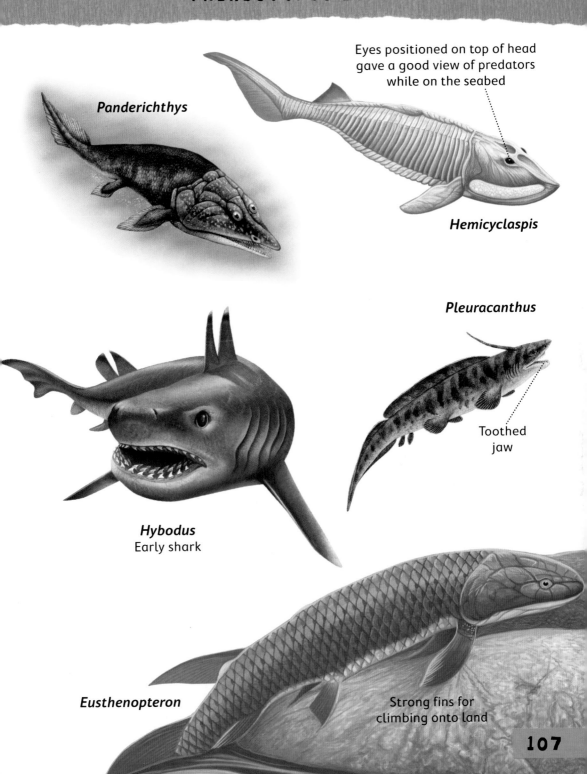

Panderichthys

Eyes positioned on top of head
gave a good view of predators
while on the seabed

Hemicyclaspis

Pleuracanthus

Toothed
jaw

Hybodus
Early shark

Eusthenopteron

Strong fins for
climbing onto land

107

Amphibians

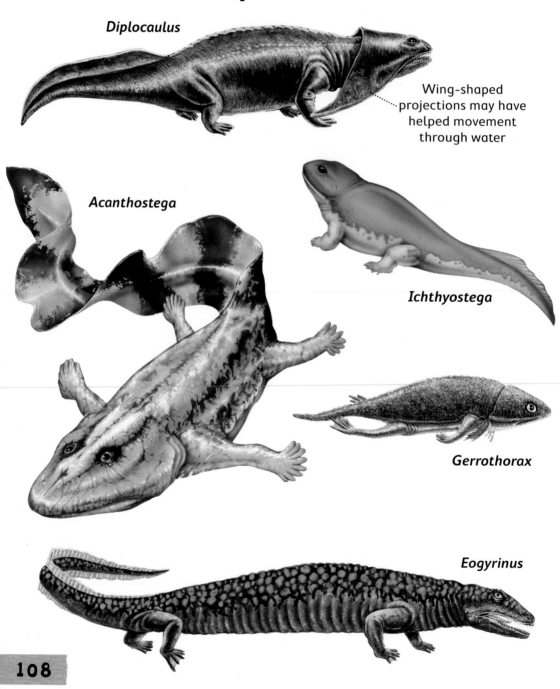

Diplocaulus

Wing-shaped projections may have helped movement through water

Acanthostega

Ichthyostega

Gerrothorax

Eogyrinus

108

Triadobatrachus

Acanthostega fossil

Mastodonsaurus

109

Land reptiles

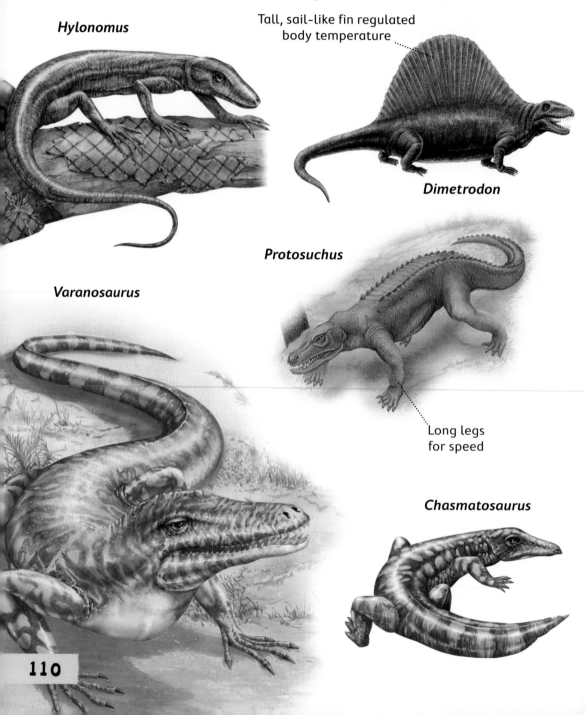

Hylonomus

Tall, sail-like fin regulated
body temperature

Dimetrodon

Protosuchus

Varanosaurus

Long legs
for speed

Chasmatosaurus

110

Lystrosaurus

Cynognathus

Fur-covered body

Strong jaws, powerful enough to bite through bone

Diictodon

Moschops

Coelurosauravus

Marine reptiles

Archelon
Similar to modern
leatherback turtles

Pteranodon snatching up
prey from the water

Elasmosaurus

Mosasaurus
Relative of modern
monitor lizards

Paddle-
shaped limbs

Proganochelys
Ancestor of modern
turtles and tortoises

Dinosaur anatomy

Dinosaurs are divided into two groups –
ornithischians (bird-hipped) and
saurischians (lizard-hipped)

Ilium

Ischium

Pubis

**Lizard-hipped
dinosaur**

Ilium

Pubis

Bird-hipped dinosaur

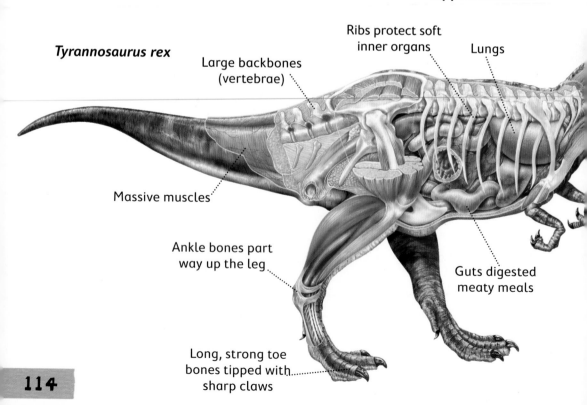

Tyrannosaurus rex

Ribs protect soft
inner organs

Lungs

Large backbones
(vertebrae)

Massive muscles

Ankle bones part
way up the leg

Guts digested
meaty meals

Long, strong toe
bones tipped with
sharp claws

114

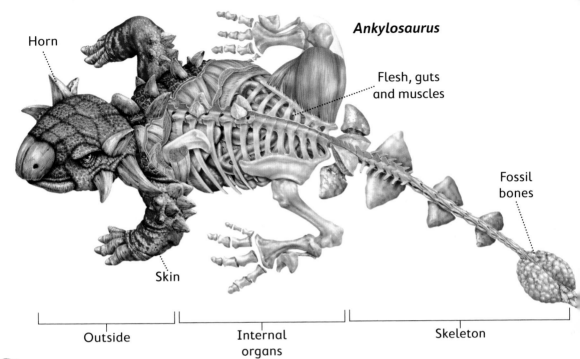

Ankylosaurus

Horn

Flesh, guts and muscles

Fossil bones

Skin

Outside

Internal organs

Skeleton

Large snout

Dinosaur skulls
By examining the teeth on dinosaur skulls, we can discover what each type of dinosaur ate

Tyrannosaurus rex
Meat eater

Sharp, knife-like teeth for tearing meat

Apatosaurus
Plant eater

Thin, blunt teeth helped pull leaves from branches

115

Attack

Some dinosaurs were equipped with speed and weapons to make them expert predators

Velociraptor
A fast, powerful and agile predator

Large nostrils indicate a good sense of smell

Tyrannosaurus rex
This large dinosaur was an expert hunter

Teeth grew up to 30 cm in length

116

Troodon
These small predatory dinosaurs may have hunted in groups

Deinonychus claws

Maiasaura

Deinonychus
Probably leapt onto its prey to attack it

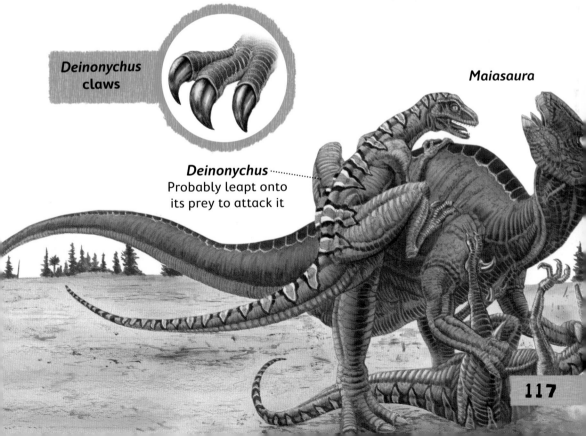

Defence

The bodies of some dinosaurs were adapted to provide them with protection from attack

Triceratops defending against Tyrannosaurus rex

Dinosaur skin

Certain types of dinosaur had armoured skins

Saltasaurus

Large bony plates

Cone-shaped plates

Scutes (bony plates in the skin) and nodules

Sauropelta

Scelidosaurus

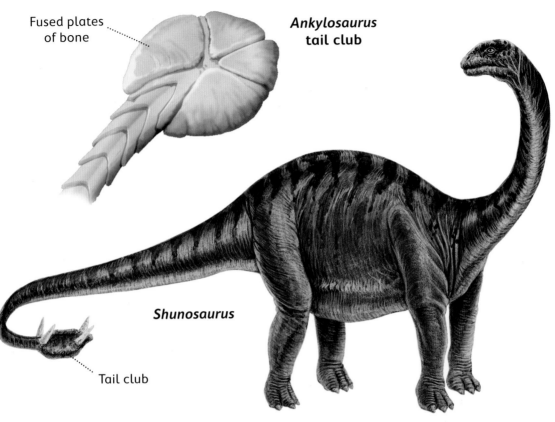

Fused plates of bone

Ankylosaurus tail club

Shunosaurus

Tail club

Ceratopsia

A group of dinosaurs with distinctive neck frills, horned faces and parrot-like beaks

Styracosaurus

Chasmosaurus

Triceratops

Triassic dinosaurs

220–203 mya

Plateosaurus
(plate-e-o-SAW-rus)

Herrerasaurus
(huh-RARE-uh-SAW-rus)

Melanorosaurus
(me-lan-or-oh-SAW-rus)

Riojasaurus
(ree-O-ha-SAW-rus)

Massospondylus
(mass-oh-SPON-di-luss)

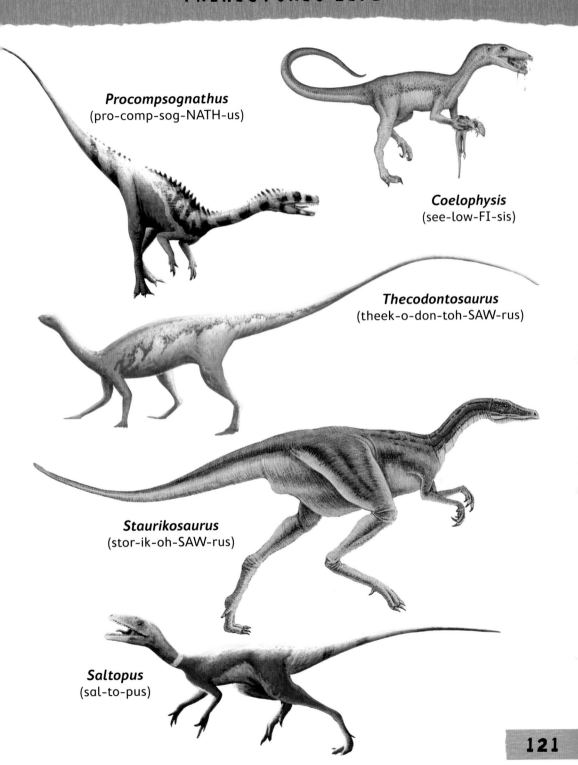

Procompsognathus
(pro-comp-sog-NATH-us)

Coelophysis
(see-low-FI-sis)

Thecodontosaurus
(theek-o-don-toh-SAW-rus)

Staurikosaurus
(stor-ik-oh-SAW-rus)

Saltopus
(sal-to-pus)

121

Jurassic dinosaurs

200–135 mya

Dilophosaurus
(die-LOAF-o-SAW-rus)

Ceratosaurus
(sir-RAT-oh-saw-rus)

Ornitholestes
(or-ni-thoe-
LESS-tees)

Barosaurus
(bare-o-SAW-rus)

Compsognathus
(komp-sog-NATH-us)

Kentrosaurus
(ken-TROH-saw-rus)

Diplodocus
(DI-plod-oh-kuss)

122

Brachiosaurus
(brack-ee-o-SAW-rus)

Eustreptospondylus
(u-STREP-toe-spon-DI-lus)

Coelurus
(seel-YEW-rus)

Tuojiangosaurus
(Two-oh-jee-ang-oh-SAW-rus)

Anchisaurus
(ANK-ee-saw-rus)

Apatosaurus
(ah-PAT-o-SAW-rus)

Allosaurus
(AL-o-saw-rus)

Yunnanosaurus
(yoo-nahn-oh-SAW-rus)

Cretaceous dinosaurs

120—65 mya

Parasaurolophus
(pa-ra-saw-ROL-off-us)

Polacanthus
(pol-a-KAN-thus)

Protoceratops
(pro-toe-SAIR-o-tops)

Giganotosaurus
(jig-an-o-toe-SAW-rus)

Stegosaurus
(steg-o-SAW-rus)

Troodon
(true-don)

Triceratops
(try-SAIR-o-tops)

Deinonychus
(die-NON-ee-kuss)

Argentinosaurus
(AR-gent-eeno-saw-rus)

124

Tyrannosaurus rex
(tie-RAN-o-SAW-rus)

Lambeosaurus
(lam-bee-o-
SAW-rus)

Struthiomimus
(STRUTH-ee-oh-
MEEM-us)

Saltasaurus
(salt-ah-SAW-rus)

Ankylosaurus
(an-KIE-low-saw-rus)

Spinosaurus
(spin-o-SAW-rus)

Baryonyx
(bare-ee-ON-ix)

Edmontonia
(ed-mon-TOE-
nee-uh)

Albertosaurus
(al-BERT-oh-saw-rus)

Birds

Confuciusornis
The first known bird to
have a true bird-like beak

Sharp-toothed
beak

Large
head

Ichthyornis
A prehistoric
seabird

Long tail
feathers

Argentavis
This giant bird of prey had
a wingspan similar to that
of a small plane

Hooked
beak

Titanis
The biggest flightless bird at 2.5 metres tall

Gastornis
At 2 metres tall, this giant had a head the size of a horse

Hesperornis
This large, flightless seabird was a strong swimmer

Waimanu
An early penguin-like bird

Mammals

Leptictidium
Related to moles

Potamotherium
Like modern otters

Powerful
shoulders

Two huge
teeth

Smilodon
Sabre-tooth cat

Sharp
claws

Uintatherium
The size of a large
rhinoceros

128

Hesperocyon
The first dog

Andrewsarchus
Biggest meat-eating mammal

Brown, shaggy hair

Woolly mammoth
Prehistoric elephants

Smaller ears than modern elephants

Huge, curved tusks

Long trunk

Hyracotherium
The first horse

Megazostrodon
The earliest known mammal

129

The first humans

1 *Ardipithecus ramidus*
    Extinct 4.5 mya

2 *Australopithecus afarensis*
    Extinct 3.5 mya

3 *Homo ergaster*
Extinct 1.9 mya

4 *Homo erectus*
Extinct 1.7 mya

5 *Homo heidelbergensis*
Extinct 600,000 years ago

6 *Homo neanderthalensis*
Extinct 100, 000
years ago

PLANTS

Hibiscus flower
Inside a flower there are many different parts, including the ovary and ovules

Plant groups

There are more than 400,000 different kinds of plant. Similar plant types are put together in different groups

Mosses grow in shady, damp places and do not make seeds

Algae vary from tiny, single-celled organisms to huge fronds of seaweed

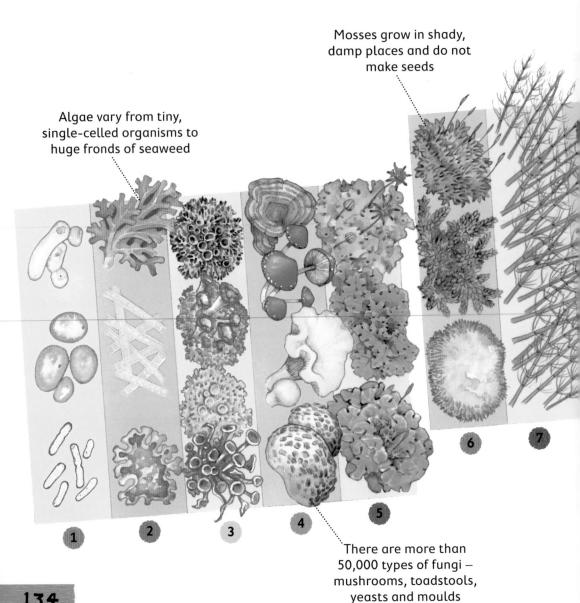

There are more than 50,000 types of fungi — mushrooms, toadstools, yeasts and moulds

134

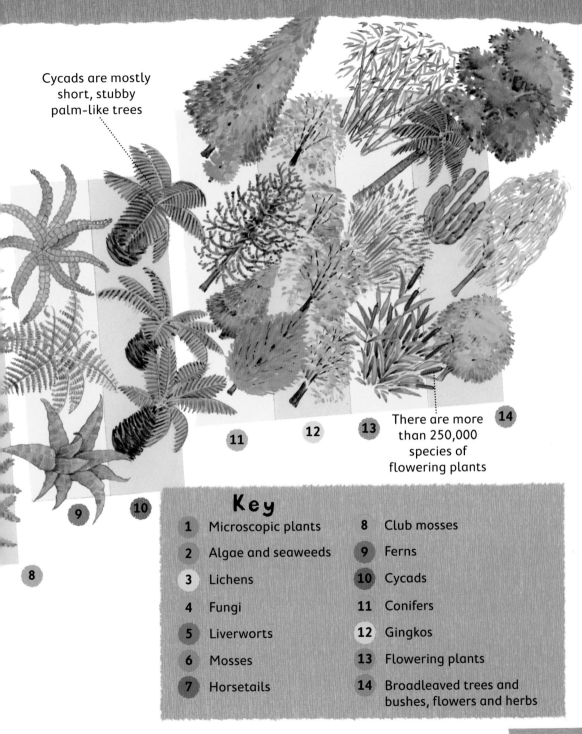

Cycads are mostly short, stubby palm-like trees

There are more than 250,000 species of flowering plants

Key

1	Microscopic plants	8	Club mosses
2	Algae and seaweeds	9	Ferns
3	Lichens	10	Cycads
4	Fungi	11	Conifers
5	Liverworts	12	Gingkos
6	Mosses	13	Flowering plants
7	Horsetails	14	Broadleaved trees and bushes, flowers and herbs

Mushrooms and toadstools

These fungi feed on plants and animals or on dead matter. Some types are poisonous so only experts should pick wild fungi

Destroying angel

Cup fungi

Stinkhorn

Chanterelle

Honey mushroom

Slimy skull cap

Ink cap

Parasol

Puffball

Field mushroom

Fairy ring mushroom

136

Fungi life cycle

Many types of fungi reproduce using spores instead of seeds

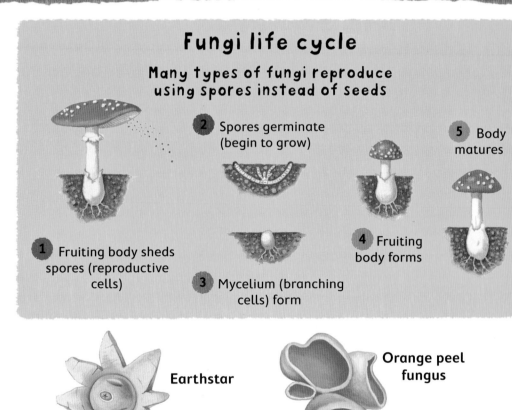

1 Fruiting body sheds spores (reproductive cells)

2 Spores germinate (begin to grow)

3 Mycelium (branching cells) form

4 Fruiting body forms

5 Body matures

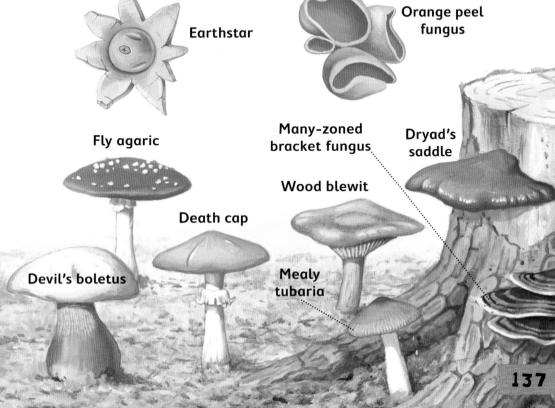

Earthstar

Orange peel fungus

Fly agaric

Many-zoned bracket fungus

Dryad's saddle

Wood blewit

Death cap

Devil's boletus

Mealy tubaria

137

Parts of a plant

Chrysanthemum
A plant that flowers
yearly (a perennial)

Bud

Flowerhead

Leaf

Stem

Roots

138

Parts of a flower

Hibiscus flower

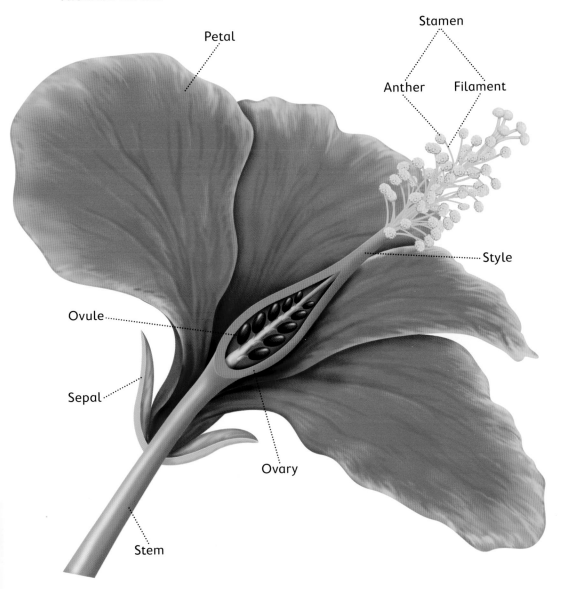

Petal

Stamen

Anther   Filament

Style

Ovule

Sepal

Ovary

Stem

Leaves

Trees can be identified by their leaves

Maple

Walnut

Willow

Horse chestnut

Raffia palm

Apple

English oak

Up close

Plants have developed many different shapes of leaf in order to survive in different conditions

Oval

Long

Hand-shaped

Compound

Needle

Inside a leaf

Waxy waterproof coat

Upper skin

Green cells

Tiny tubes inside veins supply the leaf with water

Lower skin

Carbon dioxide is taken in through pores

Inside a stem

Growing layer

Xylem vessels (tubes) carry water

Phloem vessels (tubes) carry sap

Strong internal fibres

Germination

When a seed settles in the soil, it takes in water,
swells up and opens so that the new plant can grow
— this process is called germination

Key

1. When a seed germinates, a root grows down from it and a green shoot grows up

2. The shoot grows cotyledons (seed leaves)

3. The stem and roots grow longer, and the plant begins to grow new leaves

Photosynthesis

This is the process by which most plants make food using sunlight

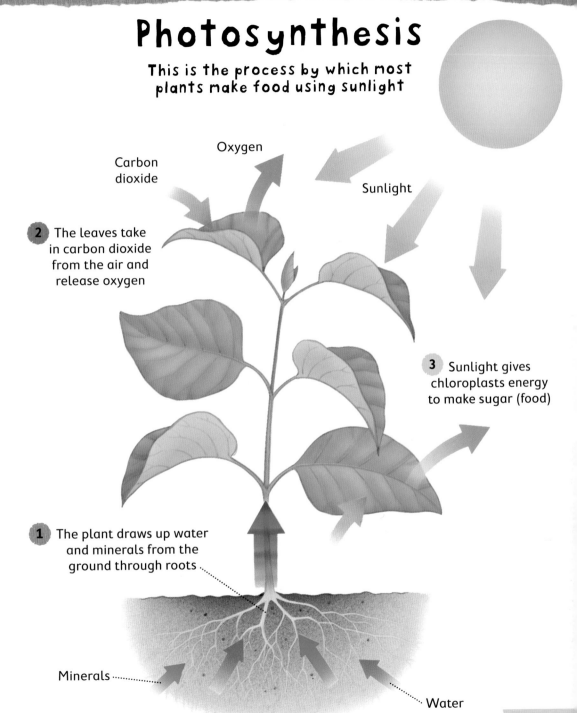

Oxygen

Carbon dioxide

Sunlight

2 The leaves take in carbon dioxide from the air and release oxygen

3 Sunlight gives chloroplasts energy to make sugar (food)

1 The plant draws up water and minerals from the ground through roots

Minerals

Water

Plant reproduction

For flowers to reproduce, male pollen needs to be delivered to the female stigma. Insects and other animals, as well as wind and water, carry pollen from flower to flower

Pollination

Bees collect pollen on their back legs. As they land on flowers, the collected pollen is transferred to flowers of the same species

Wind rocks the catkins and stamens, making the plant release its pollen

Catkins
Catkins are groups of flowers that hang down from a twig. The alder tree has male and female catkins on the same tree

Key

1 Stigma
2 Style
3 Filament
4 Anther
5 Ovule

Bee orchid
Some plants can pollinate themselves – this plant can bend to pollinate itself

Pollen cell travels down the style towards the ovule

Fertilization

1
2
4
3
5

Seeds and fruit
After pollination, the fertilized ovule develops into a seed

Mature cherry fruit contains the seed

Mosses

These are simple plants that have no flowers, true roots or leaves

Life cycle of moss
These plants reproduce from minute spores, not seeds

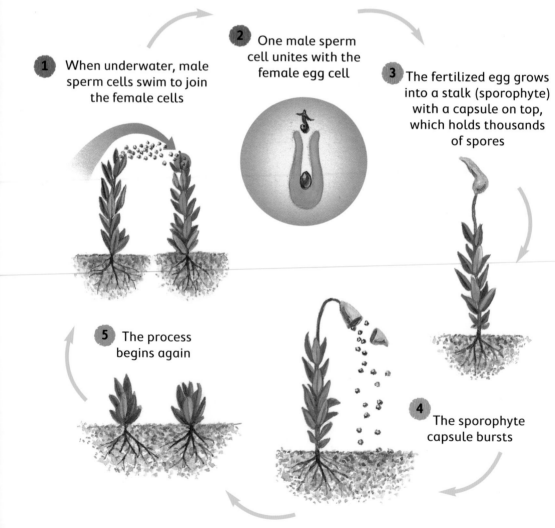

1 When underwater, male sperm cells swim to join the female cells

2 One male sperm cell unites with the female egg cell

3 The fertilized egg grows into a stalk (sporophyte) with a capsule on top, which holds thousands of spores

5 The process begins again

4 The sporophyte capsule bursts

146

Carnivorous plants

Plants that trap insects for food

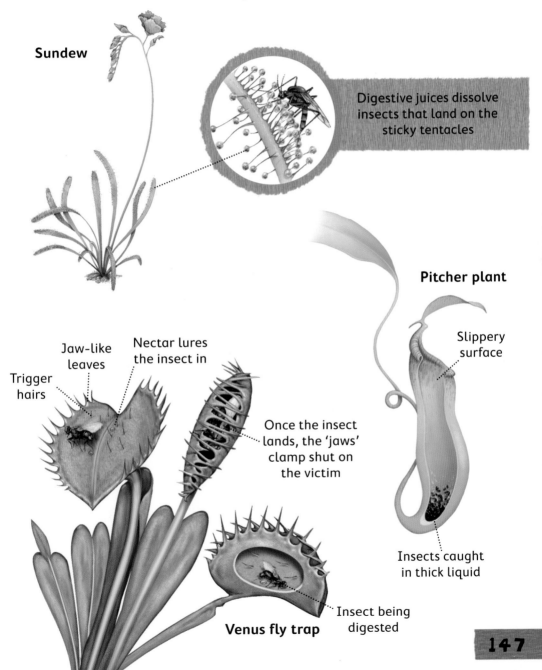

Sundew

Digestive juices dissolve insects that land on the sticky tentacles

Pitcher plant

Slippery surface

Trigger hairs

Jaw-like leaves

Nectar lures the insect in

Once the insect lands, the 'jaws' clamp shut on the victim

Insects caught in thick liquid

Insect being digested

Venus fly trap

147

Plant defences

Pebble plants
Thick, round leaves that look like pebbles provide camouflage

Water hemlock
Contains poisonous toxins

Prickly pear
Sharp spines prevent animals from reaching the water stored in the stems

Flowers

Thick, waxy skin

Spines

Nettle
Stinging hairs provide protection from animals

148

Primitive plants

Simple plants that have been around for millions of years

Tree fern

Maidenhair fern

Fern leaves are called fronds

Liverwort

Horsetail

Fern

Young fronds are curled up

Rhizome (stem) is underground

Seaweeds

Types of plants called algae that grow in the sea

Sea lettuce

Oarweed

Leaves are
transparent ·······
(see-through)

Holdfast secures
seaweed to rocks

Air bladders keep
the seaweed afloat ·······
in water

Bladderwrack

Knotted wrack

Polysiphonia, a type of red seaweed, often grows on knotted wrack

Dulse

Zones
Different seaweeds grow in different zones of a rocky seashore

Green wrack seaweeds are found on the upper intertidal zone

Brown seaweeds grow in the mid intertidal zone

Red seaweeds grow in the lower intertidal zone

151

Grasses

Plants with long, narrow leaves and small, fibrous roots that often grow wild

Bamboo

Blue gramma grass

Common cordgrass

Marram grass

152

Red oat grass

Dallas grass

Spinifex

Crested wheat grass

American prairie (grassland)

Needlegrass

Idaho fescue

Panicgrass

Switchgrass

Herbs

These plants are often used in cooking and as medicines

Dill

Thyme

Mint

Rosemary

Sage

Chives

Basil

Parsley

Bay

Fennel

Chive

Delicate pink flowerhead

Curly fronds on bright green leaves

Parsley

Small, white flowers

Rosemary

Shrubs

Small, tree-like plants with woody stems and several branches, spreading out near to the ground

Cone-shaped flowerhead made up of tiny flowers

Buddleia

Woody stem

Fragrant flowers

Berries ripen in autumn

Pink flowers with five petals

Dog rose

Pointed pairs of leaves

Honeysuckle

Egg-shaped hips (fruit)

Green-purple prickly stem

Bramble

Pink or white flowers with thorny stems. Blackberries are the shrub's fruit

Blackthorn

The fruit of this plant are dark, bitter-tasting sloes

Round, hairy leaves have pointed tips and green husks protect the nut

Hazel

Catkins are the male part. The female part looks similar to leaf buds with tiny red tassels

Garden flowers

Flowers that are planted and grown (cultivated) in gardens

Primrose

Hosta

Flowers grow from
the base of the plant
on long stalks

Clematis

Geranium

Sunflower

Hollyhock

Foxglove

Tulip

Bulb

Snowdrop

Flowers hang, or droop, from stems

Wildflowers

Yellow iris

Great
willowherb

Marsh
cinquefoil

Bluebell

Devil's-bit
scabious

Chamomile

Indian balsam

Bee orchid

Pheasant's eye

Meadowsweet

Poppy

Meadow crane's bill

Coastal flowers

Sea pea

Sea aster

Sea kale plant

Clusters of white flowers

Large, thick leaves are green or purple

Silverweed
This creeping plant grows near coasts and other damp, grassy places

Thrift

Scarlet pimpernel
Often found on sand dunes, this flower also grows on open areas and grassland

Flowerheads have bright scarlet petals

Evergreen trees
Trees that keep their leaves all year round

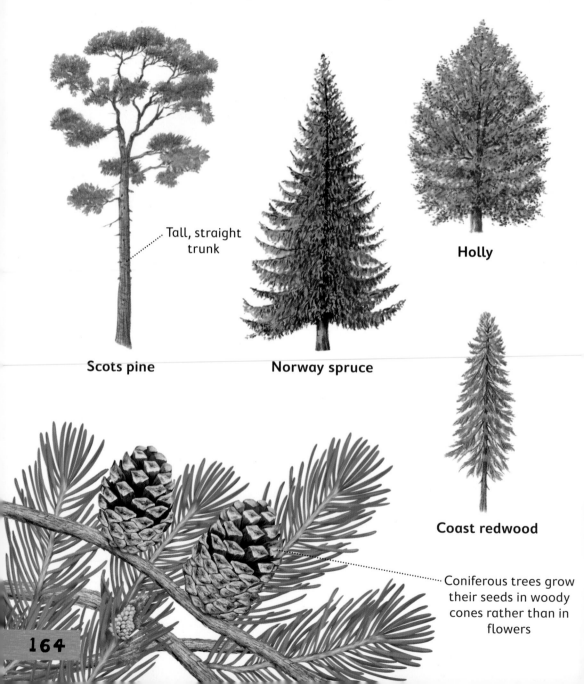

Tall, straight trunk

Holly

Scots pine

Norway spruce

Coast redwood

Coniferous trees grow their seeds in woody cones rather than in flowers

164

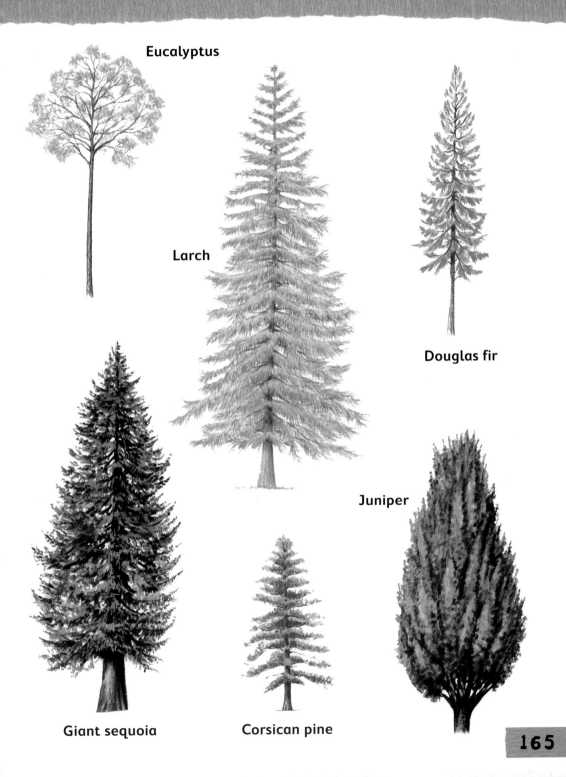

Eucalyptus

Larch

Douglas fir

Juniper

Giant sequoia

Corsican pine

Deciduous trees
Trees that drop their leaves every autumn

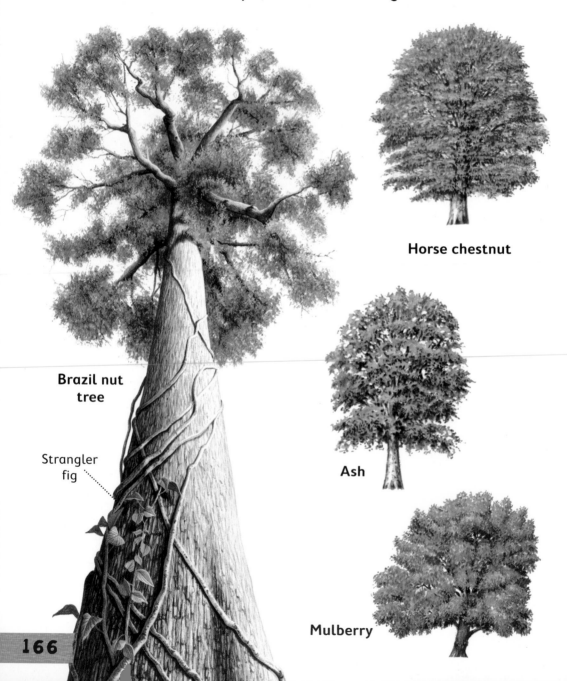

Horse chestnut

Brazil nut
tree

Strangler
fig

Ash

Mulberry

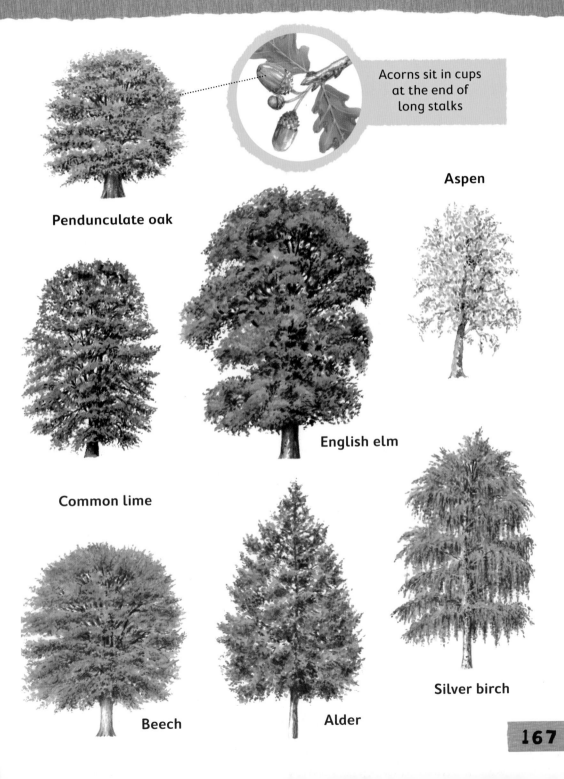

Acorns sit in cups at the end of long stalks

Pendunculate oak

Aspen

English elm

Common lime

Silver birch

Beech

Alder

Red-eyed tree frogs
These brightly coloured
creatures belong to the
amphibian animal group

ANIMALS

Molluscs

This animal group includes gastropods (such as snails), bivalves (such as mussels) and cephalopods (such as squid). All types lack backbones but some have a hard outer shell to protect their soft bodies

Gastropods

These molluscs live on land and in the sea

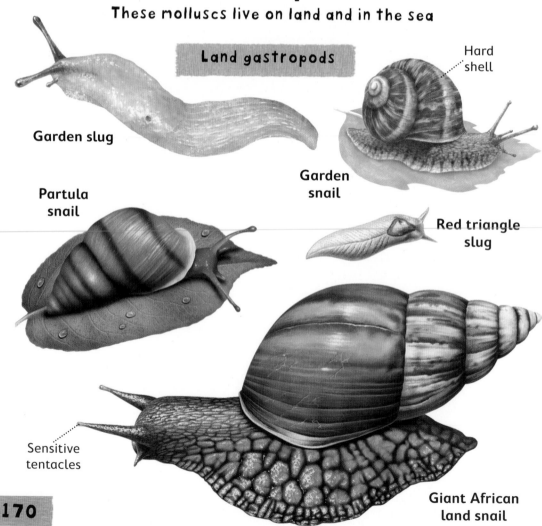

Land gastropods

Hard shell

Garden slug

Garden snail

Partula snail

Red triangle slug

Sensitive tentacles

Giant African land snail

MOLLUSCS

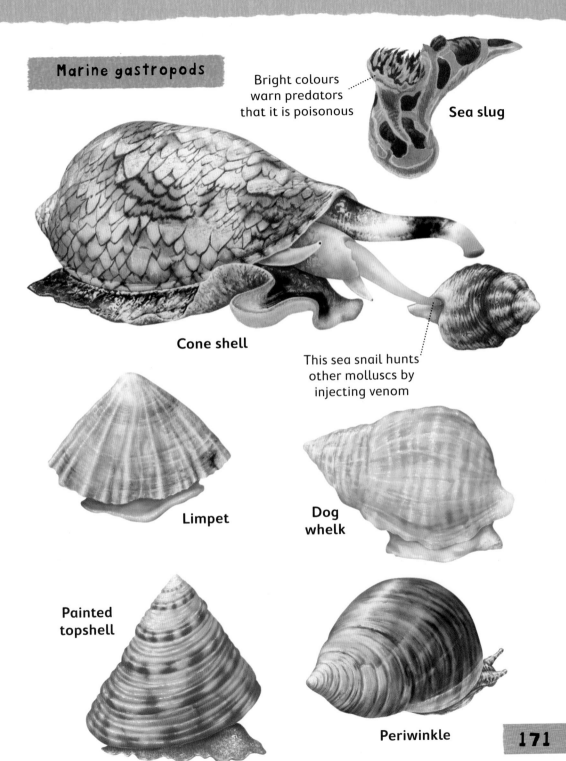

Marine gastropods

Bright colours warn predators that it is poisonous

Sea slug

Cone shell

This sea snail hunts other molluscs by injecting venom

Limpet

Dog whelk

Painted topshell

Periwinkle

Bivalves

The species in this mollusc group have two
hinged shells that can open and close

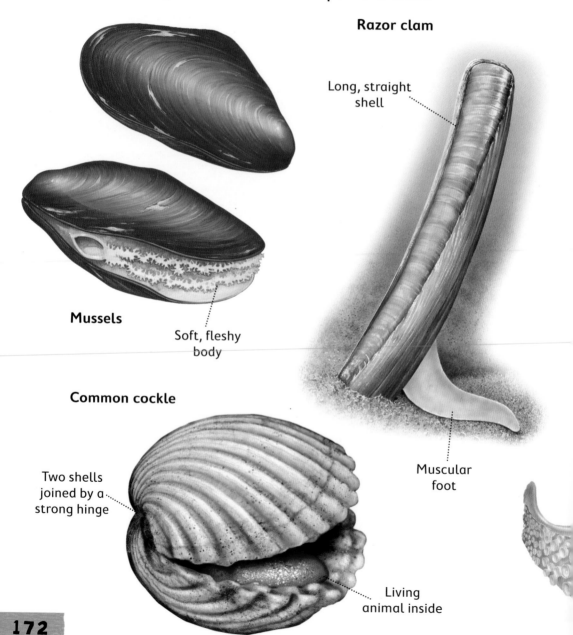

Razor clam

Long, straight
shell

Mussels

Soft, fleshy
body

Common cockle

Two shells
joined by a
strong hinge

Muscular
foot

Living
animal inside

Cephalopods

This group includes squid, octopus and cuttlefish.
Each has eight arms

Bobtail squid

Cuttlefish

Beak

Giant squid

Huge eye

Blue-ringed octopus

Arm

Tentacle

Sucker lined with teeth

Arachnids

Spiders, scorpions, ticks and mites belong to a group of animals called arachnids. All members of this animal group have eight legs. Almost all types live on land and hunt other animals to eat

Spiders

About 40,000 types of spider have been named so far, here are some example species

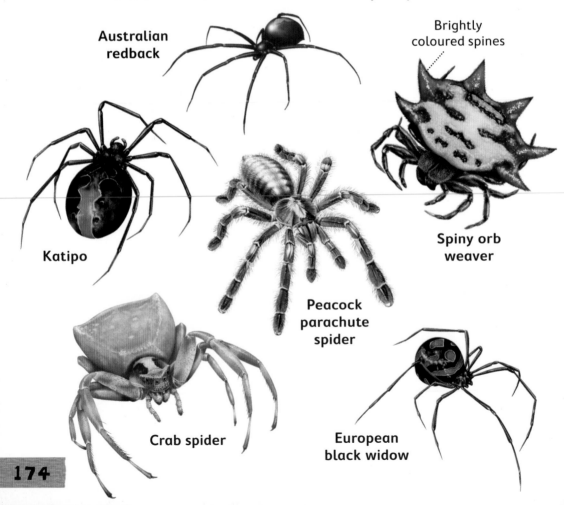

Australian redback

Brightly coloured spines

Katipo

Spiny orb weaver

Peacock parachute spider

Crab spider

European black widow

ARACHNIDS

Ladybird spiders

Female

Male

Mexican red-kneed tarantula

Hairy legs

Cobalt blue tarantula

Sydney funnel-web

Long, sharp fangs

Goliath bird-eater

Spider anatomy

Spitting spider

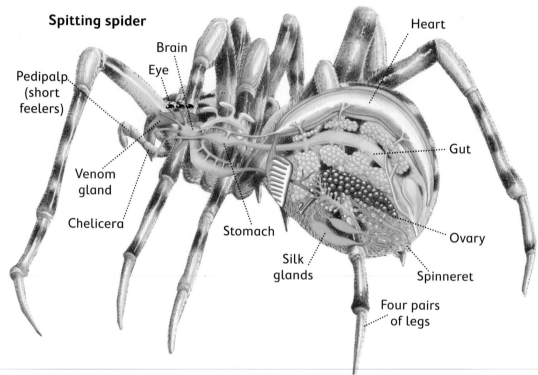

Pedipalp
(short
feelers)

Brain

Eye

Heart

Venom
gland

Chelicera

Stomach

Silk
glands

Gut

Ovary

Spinneret

Four pairs
of legs

Spinnerets
Produce silk

Spigots produce
coarse silk for
making webs

Spools produce fine
silk for wrapping prey

176

Claw

Foot
The underside is covered in hairs. Each hair is split into microscopic end-feet, which allow spiders to grip surfaces

Tufts of hair, called scopulae

Eyes
Most spiders have eight eyes, which are arranged in two or three rows at the front of the head

Jumping spider

Ogre-faced spider

Main eyes can see images in focus and with detail

Side eyes spot movement

Spitting spider

Crab spider

177

Spider hunting behaviour

Spiders can be divided into two groups – those
that hunt their prey and those that trap it

Trapdoor spider

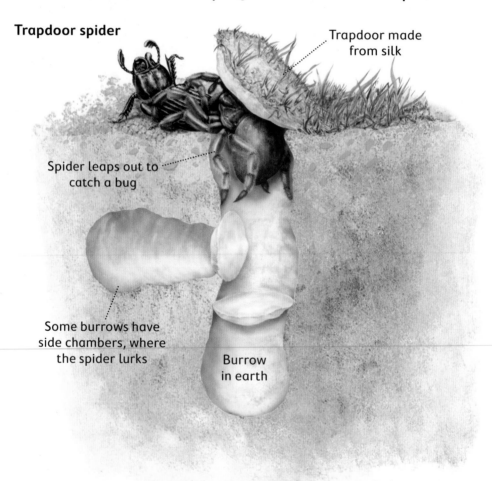

Trapdoor made
from silk

Spider leaps out to
catch a bug

Some burrows have
side chambers, where
the spider lurks

Burrow
in earth

Bolas spider

Sticky ball of silk
attaches to prey

Length of silk

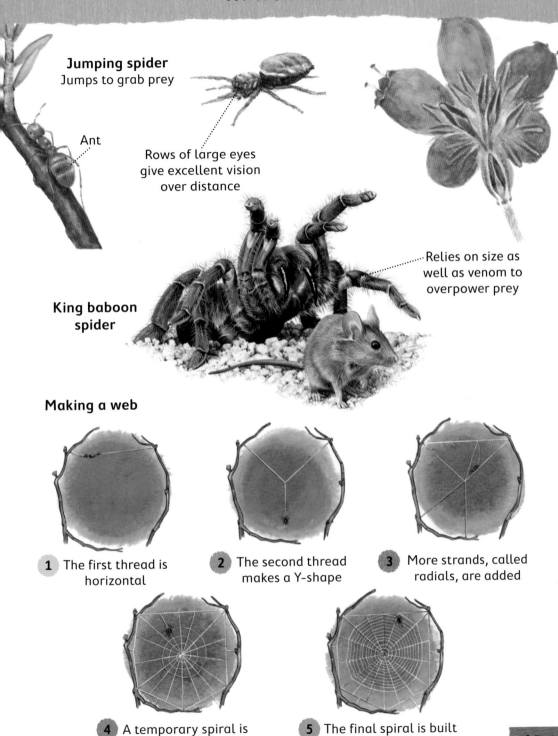

Jumping spider
Jumps to grab prey

Ant

Rows of large eyes
give excellent vision
over distance

Relies on size as
well as venom to
overpower prey

**King baboon
spider**

Making a web

1 The first thread is
horizontal

2 The second thread
makes a Y-shape

3 More strands, called
radials, are added

4 A temporary spiral is
put in place

5 The final spiral is built
more carefully

179

Scorpions

These arachnids are easily identified by the sting
at the end of their tail and their lobster-like pincers

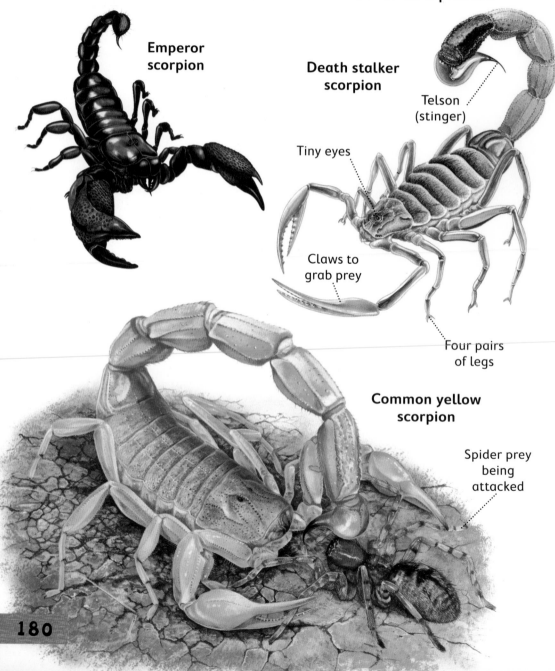

Emperor
scorpion

Death stalker
scorpion

Telson
(stinger)

Tiny eyes

Claws to
grab prey

Four pairs
of legs

Common yellow
scorpion

Spider prey
being
attacked

Other arachnids

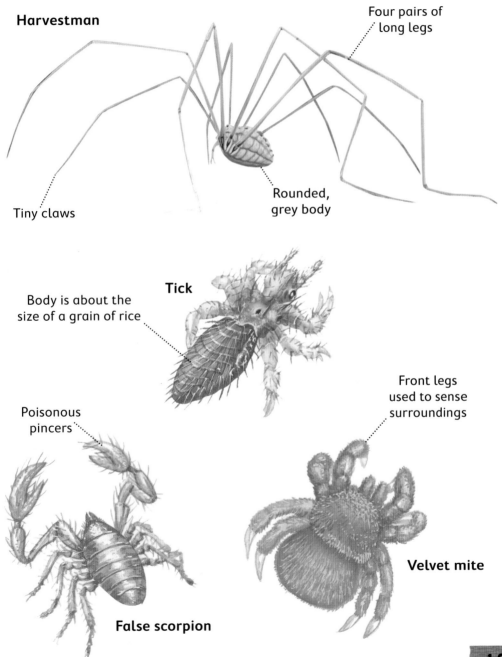

Harvestman

Four pairs of long legs

Tiny claws

Rounded, grey body

Tick

Body is about the size of a grain of rice

Front legs used to sense surroundings

Poisonous pincers

Velvet mite

False scorpion

181

Crustaceans

This animal group is mostly marine.
All have a hard outer-body casing

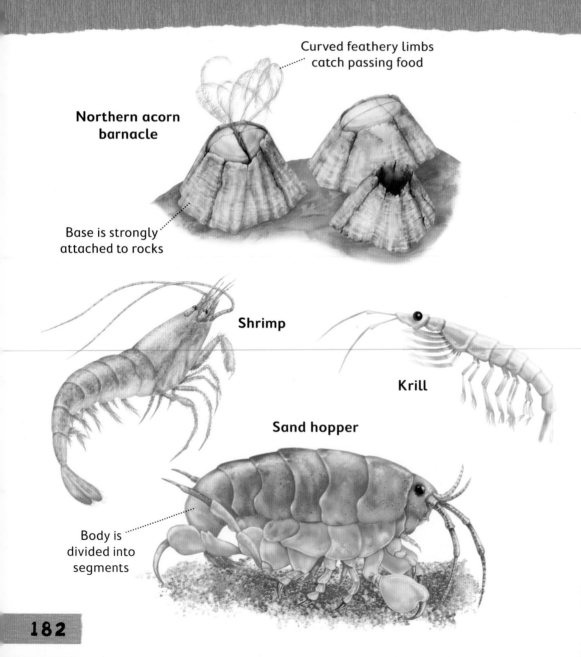

Curved feathery limbs
catch passing food

**Northern acorn
barnacle**

Base is strongly
attached to rocks

Shrimp

Krill

Sand hopper

Body is
divided into
segments

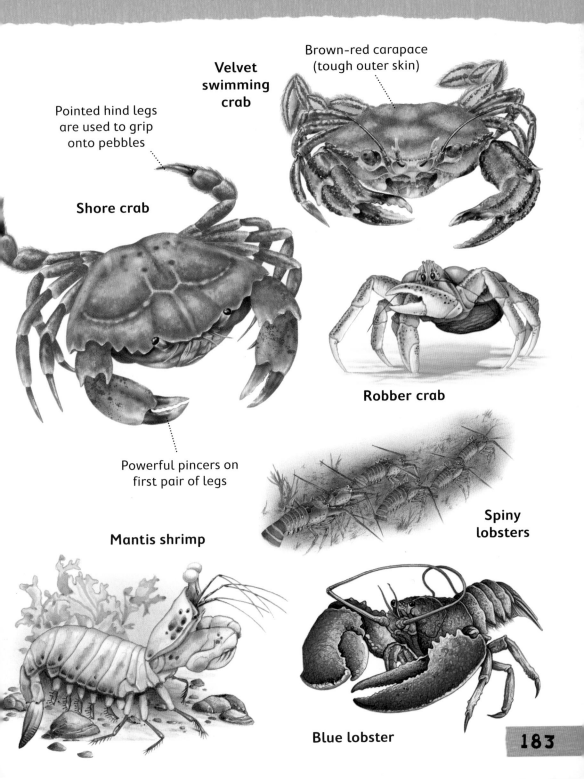

Velvet swimming crab

Brown-red carapace (tough outer skin)

Pointed hind legs are used to grip onto pebbles

Shore crab

Robber crab

Powerful pincers on first pair of legs

Mantis shrimp

Spiny lobsters

Blue lobster

183

Insects

All insects have six legs and an outer body casing called an exoskeleton. Their bodies are divided into three parts — the head, thorax (middle section) and abdomen (rear section)

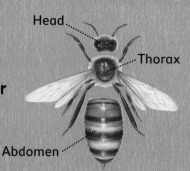

Head

Thorax

Abdomen

Flies and dragonflies

Scientists define a fly as an insect with two wings. Insects with four wings, such as dragonflies, aren't true flies

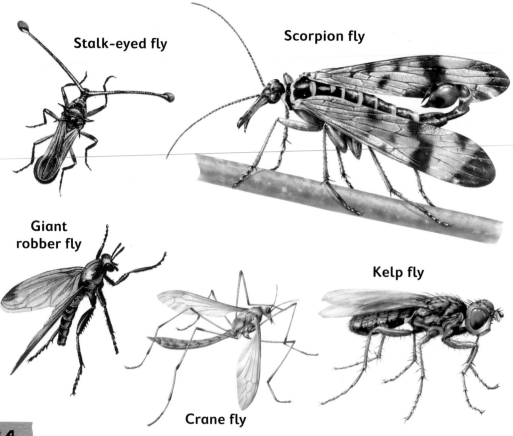

Stalk-eyed fly

Scorpion fly

Giant robber fly

Kelp fly

Crane fly

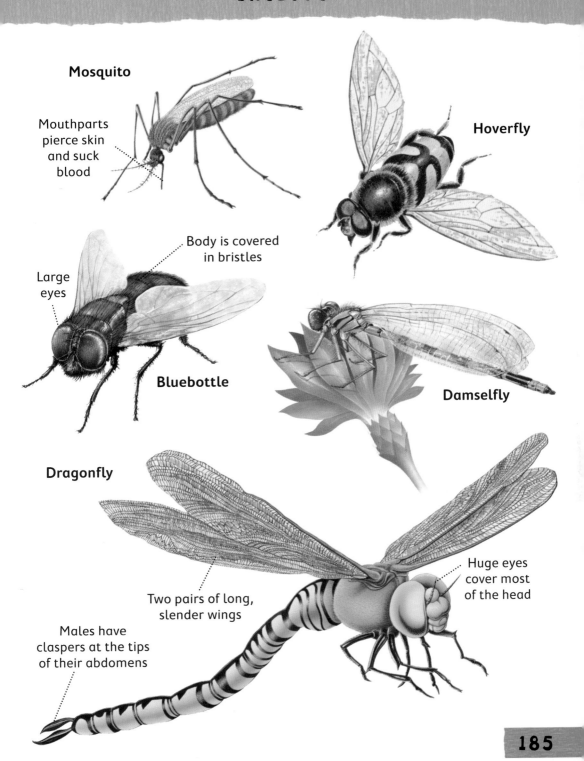

Mosquito

Mouthparts pierce skin and suck blood

Hoverfly

Body is covered in bristles

Large eyes

Bluebottle

Damselfly

Dragonfly

Two pairs of long, slender wings

Males have claspers at the tips of their abdomens

Huge eyes cover most of the head

Crickets and grasshoppers

Although most types have wings, these insects use their powerful back legs to leap away from danger

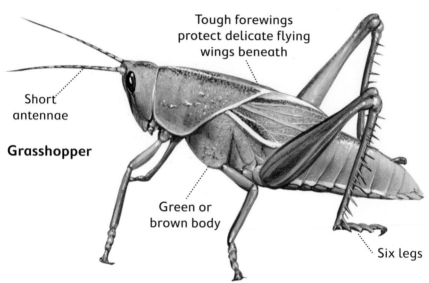

Tough forewings protect delicate flying wings beneath

Short antennae

Grasshopper

Green or brown body

Six legs

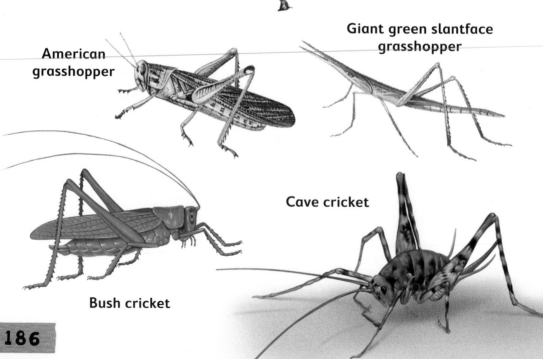

American grasshopper

Giant green slantface grasshopper

Cave cricket

Bush cricket

Mantids

These expert predators lie in wait for prey, then snatch it with their spine-studded front legs

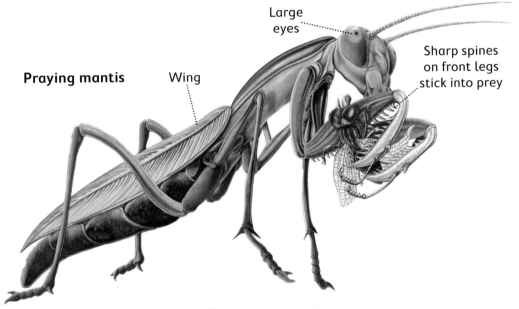

Large eyes

Sharp spines on front legs stick into prey

Praying mantis

Wing

Cockroaches

Often seen as pests, these hardy insects have changed little over the last 300 million years

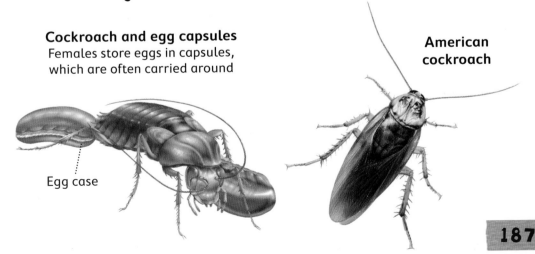

Cockroach and egg capsules
Females store eggs in capsules, which are often carried around

Egg case

American cockroach

Termites

These soft-bodied insects live in colonies that can number millions

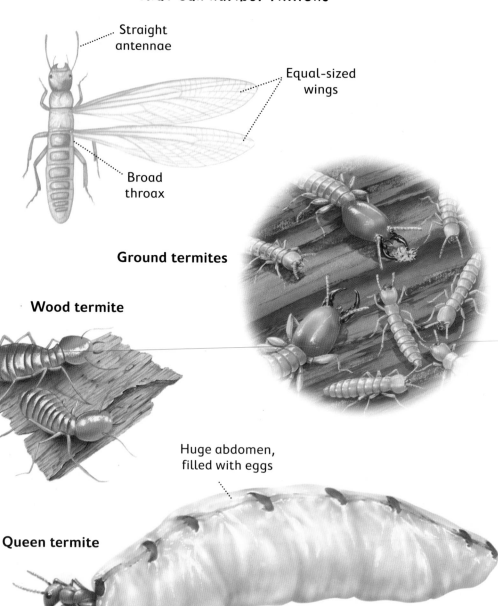

Straight antennae

Equal-sized wings

Broad throax

Ground termites

Wood termite

Huge abdomen, filled with eggs

Queen termite

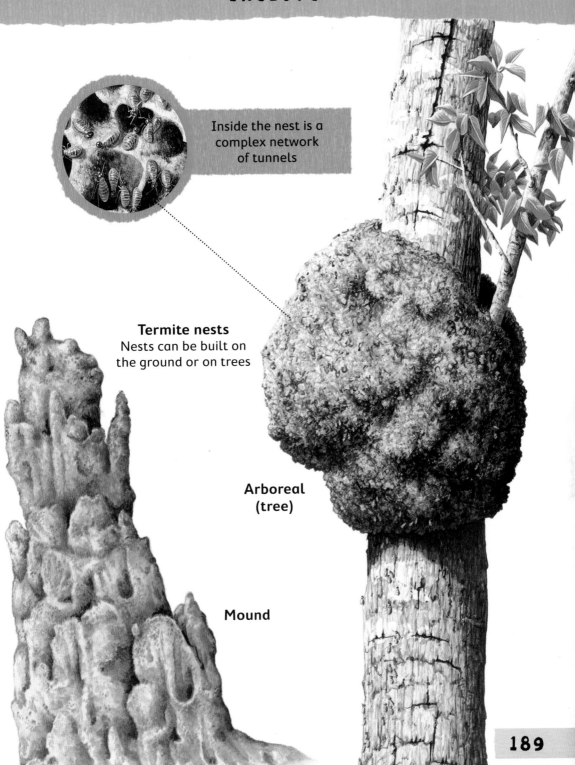

Inside the nest is a complex network of tunnels

Termite nests
Nests can be built on the ground or on trees

Arboreal (tree)

Mound

Beetles

There are at least 360,000 species of beetle, making up about one-third of all animal species

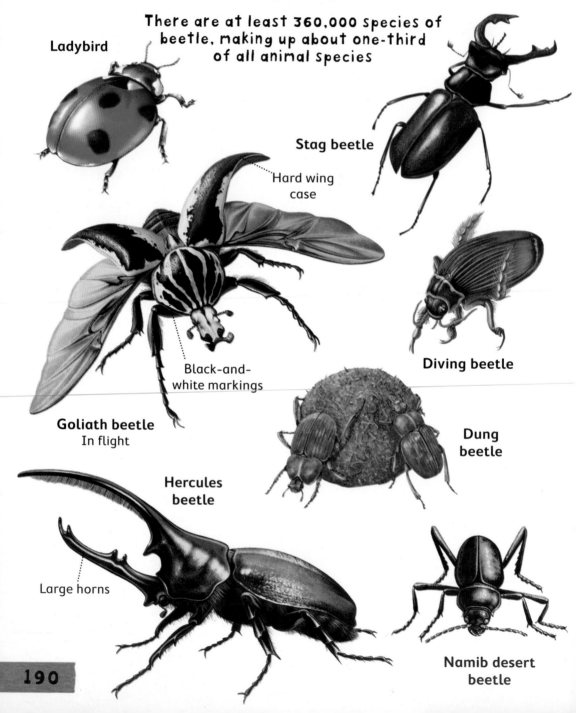

Ladybird

Stag beetle

Hard wing case

Black-and-white markings

Goliath beetle
In flight

Diving beetle

Dung beetle

Hercules beetle

Large horns

Namib desert beetle

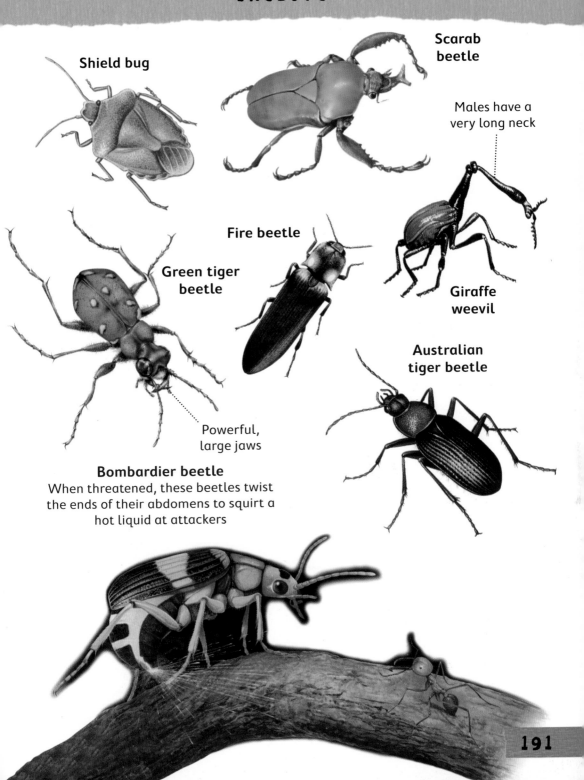

Shield bug

Scarab beetle

Males have a very long neck

Fire beetle

Green tiger beetle

Giraffe weevil

Australian tiger beetle

Powerful, large jaws

Bombardier beetle
When threatened, these beetles twist the ends of their abdomens to squirt a hot liquid at attackers

Butterflies

These pretty insects usually have delicate,
slender bodies. They mostly fly by day

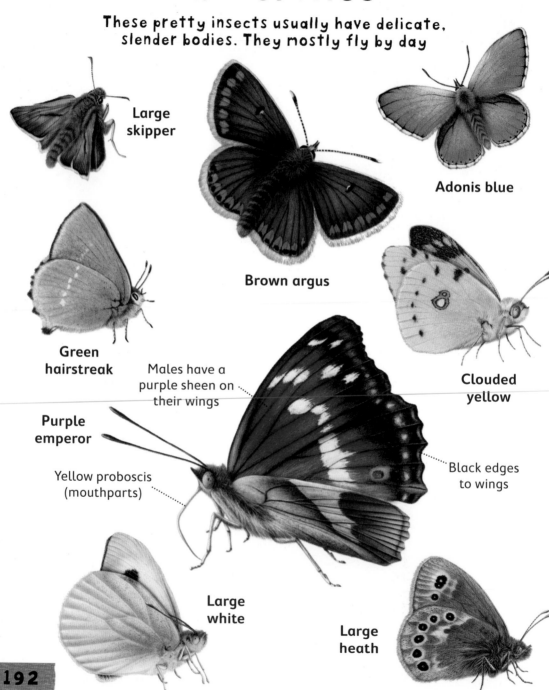

Large
skipper

Adonis blue

Brown argus

Green
hairstreak

Clouded
yellow

Males have a
purple sheen on
their wings

Purple
emperor

Black edges
to wings

Yellow proboscis
(mouthparts)

Large
white

Large
heath

192

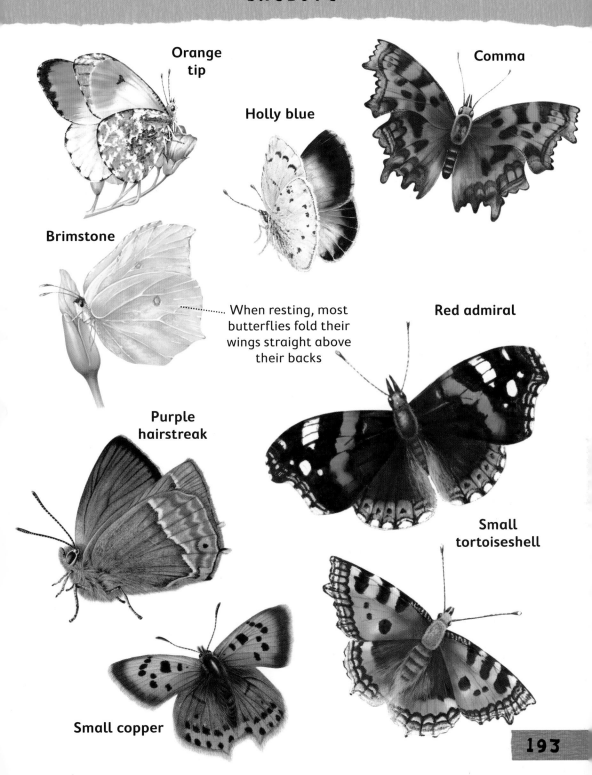

Orange tip

Comma

Holly blue

Brimstone

When resting, most butterflies fold their wings straight above their backs

Red admiral

Purple hairstreak

Small tortoiseshell

Small copper

193

Moths

Most moths are only active at night but some are active during the day

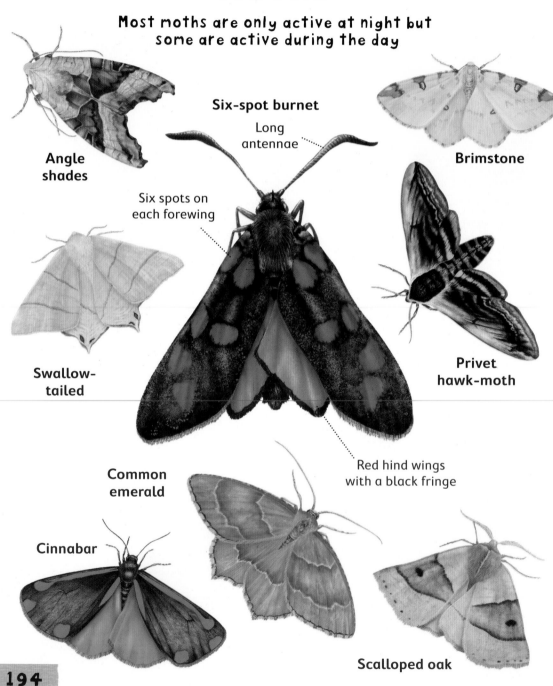

Angle shades

Six-spot burnet

Long antennae

Brimstone

Six spots on each forewing

Swallow-tailed

Privet hawk-moth

Common emerald

Cinnabar

Red hind wings with a black fringe

Scalloped oak

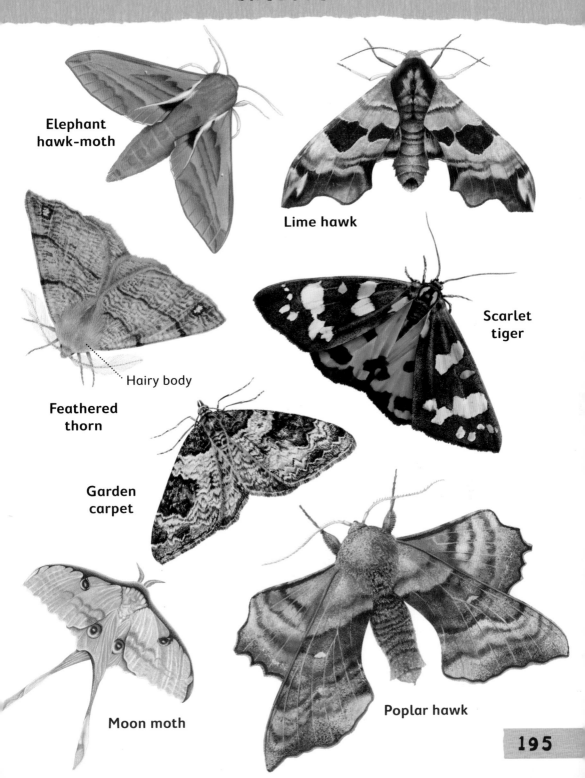

Elephant
hawk-moth

Lime hawk

Hairy body

Feathered
thorn

Scarlet
tiger

Garden
carpet

Moon moth

Poplar hawk

195

Butterfly life cycle

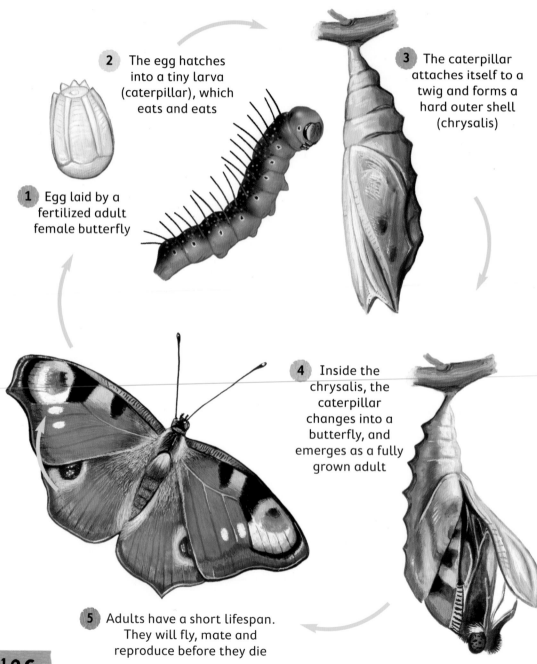

2 The egg hatches into a tiny larva (caterpillar), which eats and eats

3 The caterpillar attaches itself to a twig and forms a hard outer shell (chrysalis)

1 Egg laid by a fertilized adult female butterfly

4 Inside the chrysalis, the caterpillar changes into a butterfly, and emerges as a fully grown adult

5 Adults have a short lifespan. They will fly, mate and reproduce before they die

Caterpillars

In order to put off predators, many caterpillars
have bright colours and patterns, or even venomous hairs

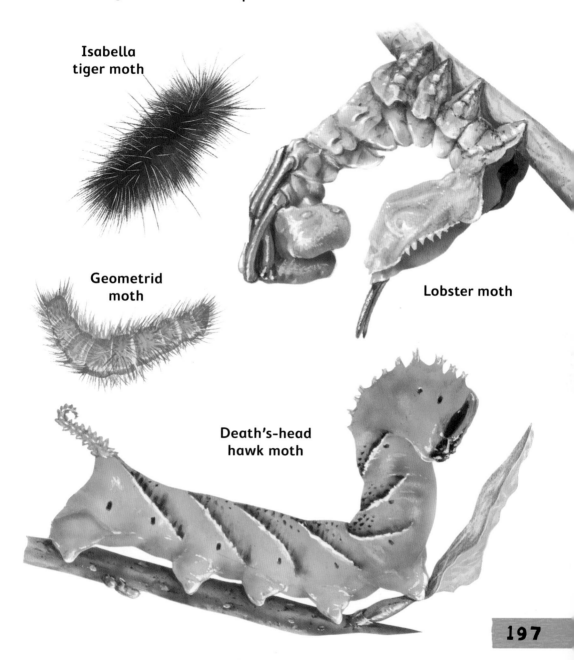

Isabella
tiger moth

Geometrid
moth

Lobster moth

Death's-head
hawk moth

Ants

Ants are social insects that live in huge colonies.
There are more than 9000 different species

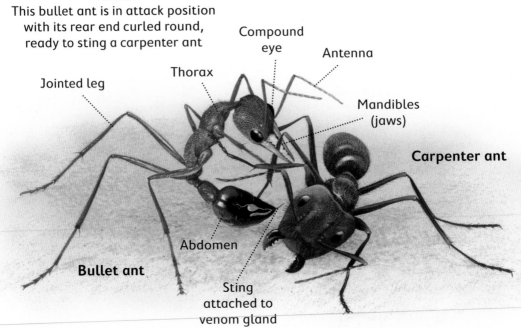

Attack
This bullet ant is in attack position
with its rear end curled round,
ready to sting a carpenter ant

Compound
eye

Antenna

Thorax

Jointed leg

Mandibles
(jaws)

Carpenter ant

Abdomen

Bullet ant

Sting
attached to
venom gland

Leafcutter ants
These ants cut and then carry
leaves back to their nest

INSECTS

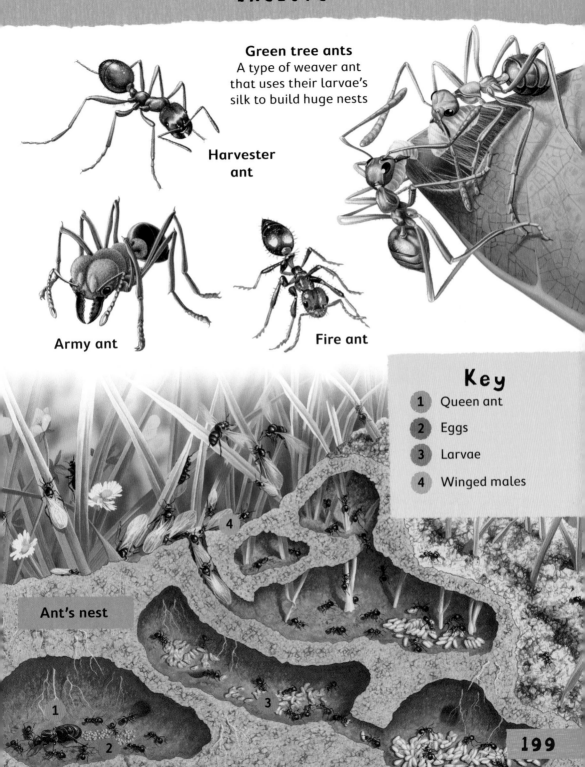

Green tree ants
A type of weaver ant that uses their larvae's silk to build huge nests

Harvester ant

Army ant

Fire ant

Key

1 Queen ant

2 Eggs

3 Larvae

4 Winged males

Ant's nest

Bees

Bees are small insects with stings that feed on pollen and nectar from flowers. Bees that live in colonies secrete wax to build their nests

Mason bee

Orchid bee

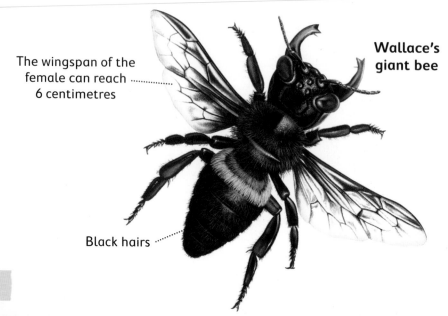

Wallace's giant bee

The wingspan of the female can reach 6 centimetres

Black hairs

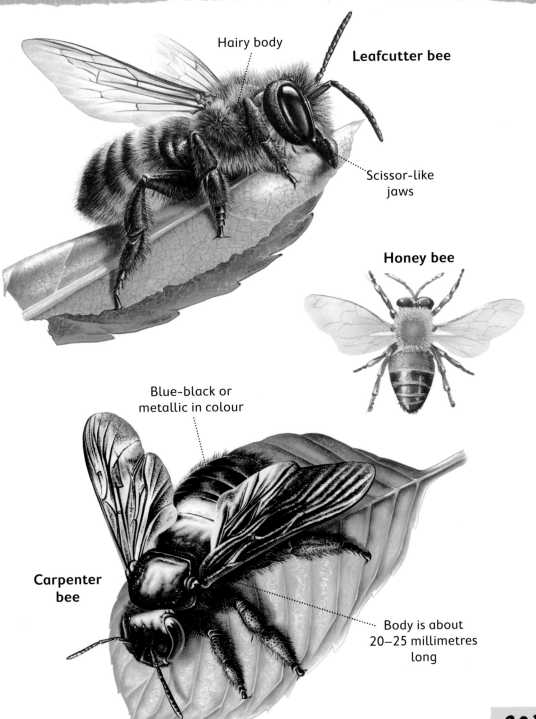

Hairy body

Leafcutter bee

Scissor-like
jaws

Honey bee

Blue-black or
metallic in colour

**Carpenter
bee**

Body is about
20–25 millimetres
long

Wasps

Wasps either live alone or in huge colonies. The adults feed on nectar, fruit and plant sap, while the larvae (young) feed on insects

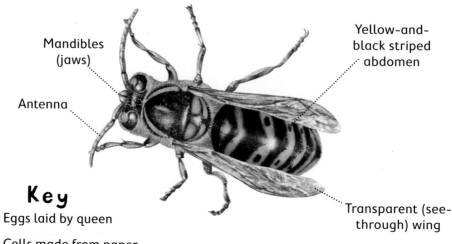

Mandibles (jaws)

Antenna

Yellow-and-black striped abdomen

Transparent (see-through) wing

Key

1 Eggs laid by queen

2 Cells made from paper

3 Wasps adding paper around the outside of the nest

Wasp nest

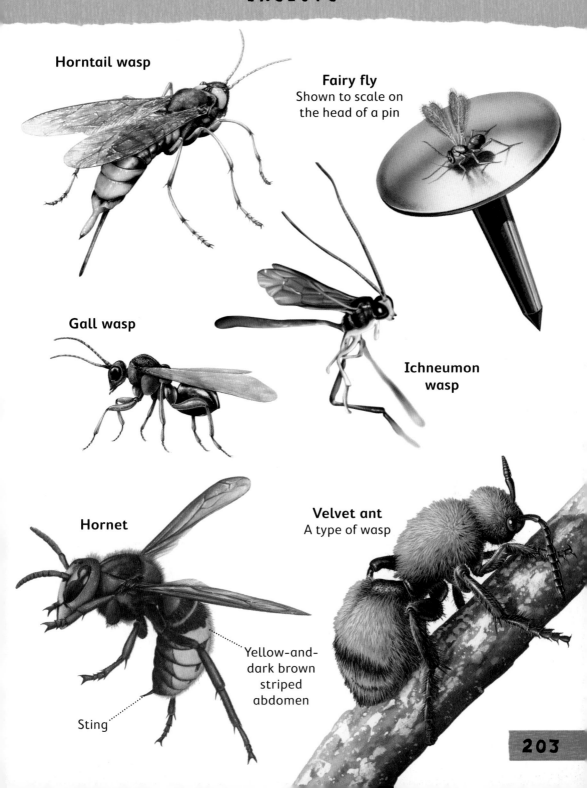

Horntail wasp

Fairy fly
Shown to scale on
the head of a pin

Gall wasp

**Ichneumon
wasp**

Hornet

Velvet ant
A type of wasp

Yellow-and-
dark brown
striped
abdomen

Sting

203

Fish

Fish are the largest group of animals
with backbones. They are mainly equipped
to live either in freshwater or in the sea

Bony fish

The biggest group of fish have
skeletons made of bone

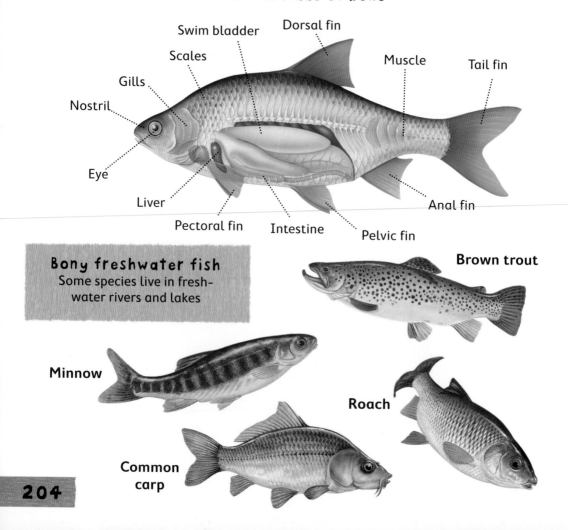

Swim bladder

Scales

Gills

Nostril

Eye

Liver

Pectoral fin

Dorsal fin

Muscle

Tail fin

Intestine

Pelvic fin

Anal fin

Bony freshwater fish
Some species live in freshwater rivers and lakes

Brown trout

Minnow

Roach

Common
carp

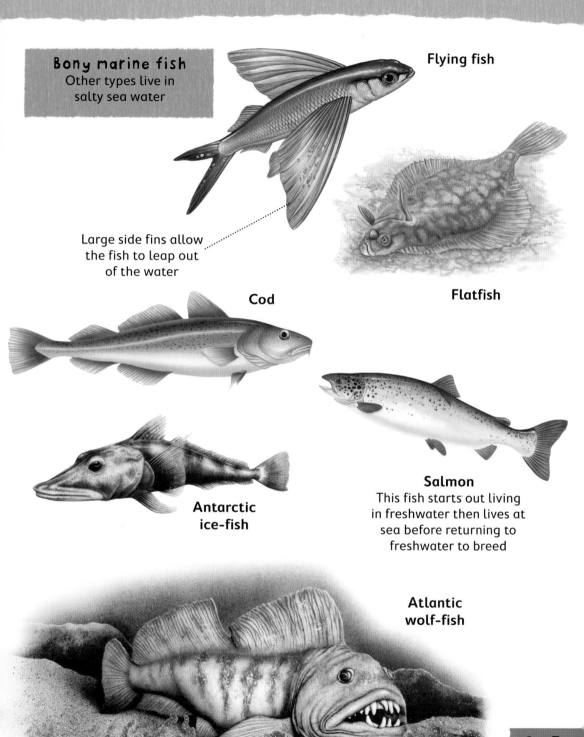

Bony marine fish
Other types live in salty sea water

Flying fish

Large side fins allow the fish to leap out of the water

Flatfish

Cod

Salmon
This fish starts out living in freshwater then lives at sea before returning to freshwater to breed

Antarctic ice-fish

Atlantic wolf-fish

205

Coral reef fish

These colourful fish live on or around coral reefs
— large marine structures made by tiny
creatures called polyps

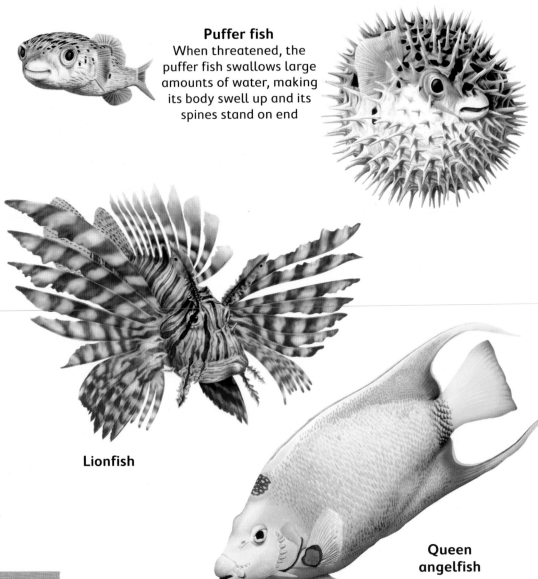

Puffer fish
When threatened, the
puffer fish swallows large
amounts of water, making
its body swell up and its
spines stand on end

Lionfish

**Queen
angelfish**

Spiny seahorse

Long tail wraps
around coral
and seaweed

**Leafy sea
dragon**

Anemone

Clownfish

207

Deep-sea fish

These fish have adapted to survive at great ocean
depths and have some very strange features

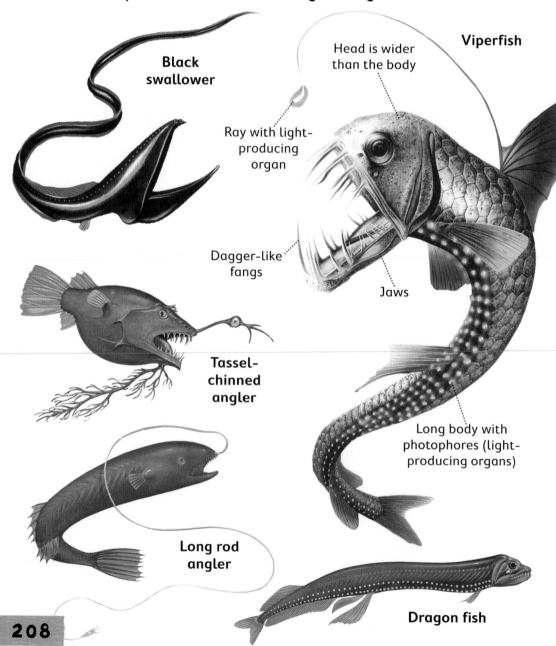

Viperfish

Black
swallower

Head is wider
than the body

Ray with light-
producing
organ

Dagger-like
fangs

Jaws

Tassel-
chinned
angler

Long body with
photophores (light-
producing organs)

Long rod
angler

Dragon fish

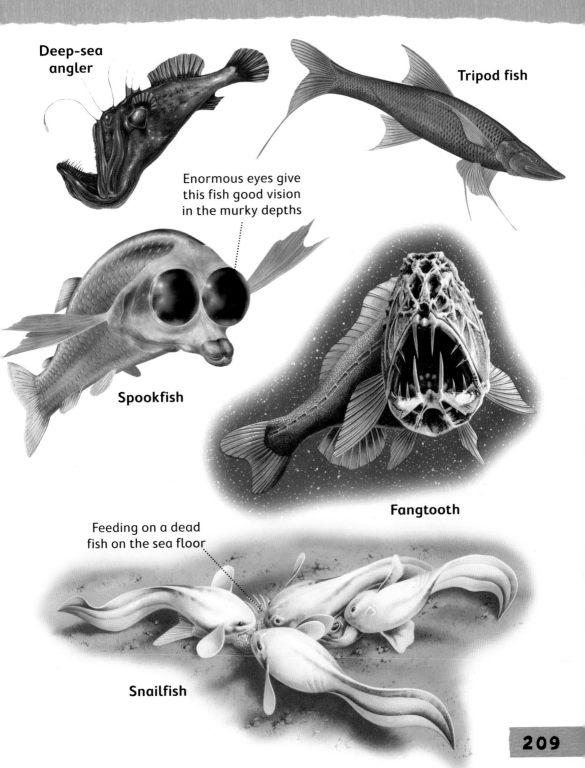

Deep-sea angler

Tripod fish

Enormous eyes give this fish good vision in the murky depths

Spookfish

Fangtooth

Feeding on a dead fish on the sea floor

Snailfish

Shark anatomy

Three groups of fish — sharks, skates and rays, and chimeras have a skeleton made of cartilage instead of bone. They are known as cartilaginous fish

Anatomy

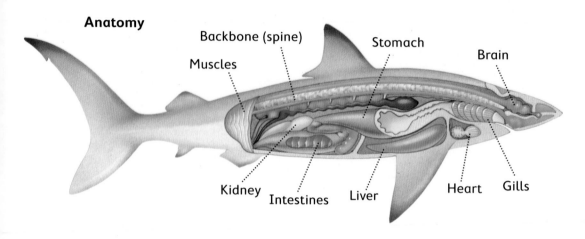

Backbone (spine)

Muscles

Stomach

Brain

Kidney

Intestines

Liver

Heart

Gills

Skeleton

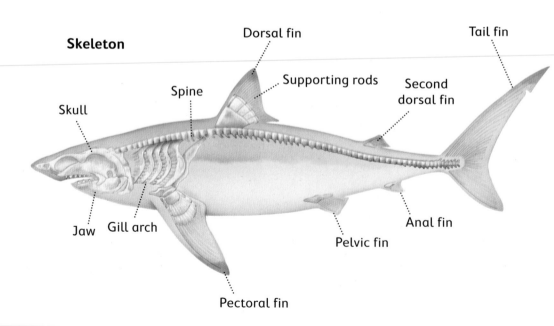

Dorsal fin

Tail fin

Spine

Supporting rods

Second dorsal fin

Skull

Jaw

Gill arch

Pelvic fin

Anal fin

Pectoral fin

Sharks

There are around 375 species (types)
of shark, living in mostly warm seas

Greenland
shark

Bonnethead
shark

Black-tip reef
shark

Lemon shark

Bramble shark

Streamlined
body

Shortfin mako
shark

Crescent-
shaped tail

211

Thresher shark

Long, whip-like tail

Tiger shark

Monk seal prey

White-tip reef shark

Cleaner wrasse fish nibble away skin, scales and pests

Goblin
shark

Long snout

Basking shark

Cookie-cutter shark

Megamouth
shark

Bull shark

Weasel shark

Great white
shark

Teeth are
large, flat and
triangular

Baby sharks

Some sharks lay eggs while others give birth to live young, called 'pups'

Egg development
A baby catshark develops
slowly in its protective case

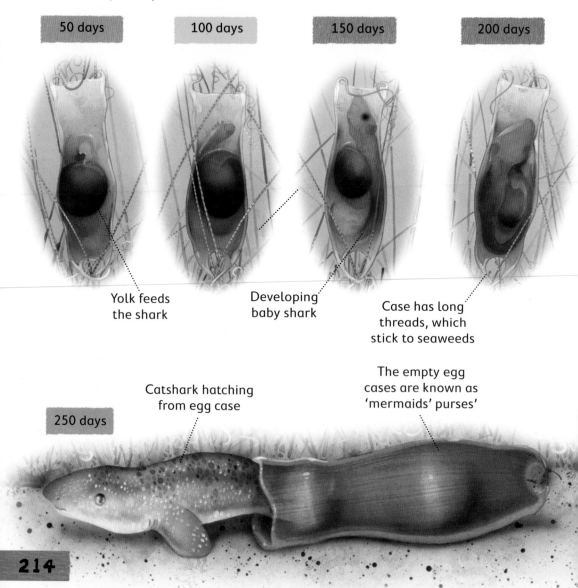

50 days

100 days

150 days

200 days

Yolk feeds
the shark

Developing
baby shark

Case has long
threads, which
stick to seaweeds

The empty egg
cases are known as
'mermaids' purses'

Catshark hatching
from egg case

250 days

Port Jackson shark laying an egg

Egg case

Lantern shark pup
A shark's egg contains a yolk that feeds the pup as it grows

Sand tiger shark pups

Shark senses

Blue shark

Electric sense
Tiny pores on the skin help sharks sense prey by picking up electrical signals

Ampullae of Lorenzini sense electricity from nearby fish

Eyesight
Deep water sharks have large eyes to allow them to see in the murky depths

Crocodile shark

Skin
Sensitive pits along the side of the body contain nerve endings that detect vibrations in the water

Lateral line

Smell
Sharks have paired nostrils, which allow them to detect scents quickly

Paired nostrils

Sand tiger shark

Shark camouflage

Many sharks have colours and patterns that help them blend into their environment

Angel shark

Mottled pattern

Spots turn to stripes as the shark matures

Zebra shark

Wobbegong

Flattened body, with lumpy, patterned skin

Skates and rays

These fish are closely related to sharks – they
have cartilage instead of bone in their skeletons

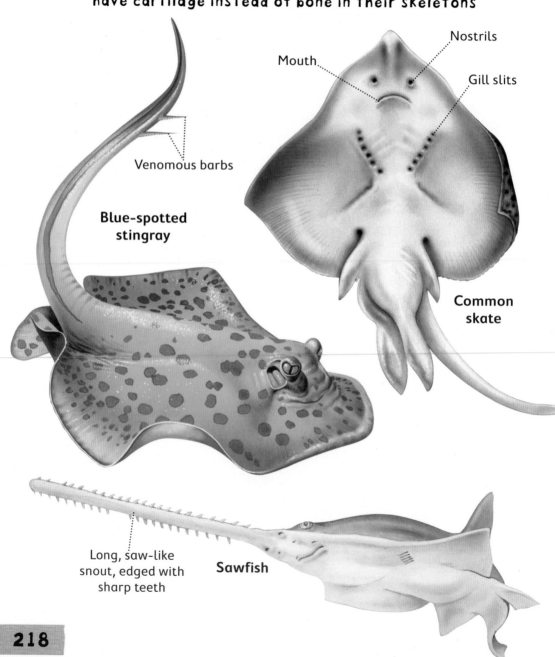

Nostrils

Mouth

Gill slits

Venomous barbs

**Blue-spotted
stingray**

**Common
skate**

Long, saw-like
snout, edged with
sharp teeth

Sawfish

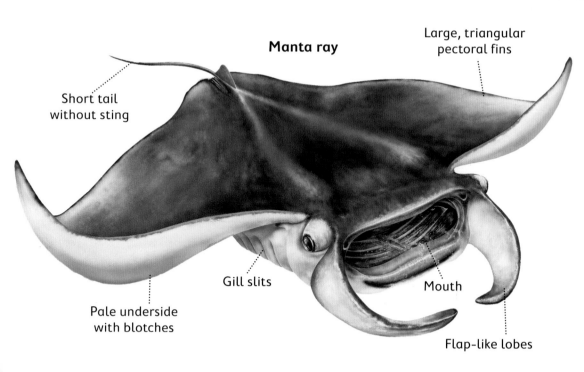

Manta ray

Short tail without sting

Large, triangular pectoral fins

Gill slits

Mouth

Pale underside with blotches

Flap-like lobes

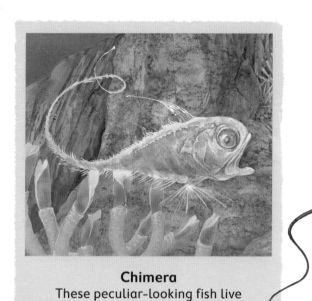

Chimera
These peculiar-looking fish live in deep water and are related to sharks, skates and rays

Spotted eagle ray

Amphibians

This animal group can live on land and in water,
and includes frogs, toads, newts, salamanders
and caecilians (worm-like animals)

Frogs

Most frogs live in damp places and tend to have
webbed feet, long back legs and smooth skin

Common frog

Rounded snout

Large black eyes flecked with gold and brown

Forelimbs are shorter than hind limbs

Hind limbs have webbed toes

Skin is moist and mottled brown and green in colour

American bullfrog

Tadpoles

Green poison dart frog

Red-eyed tree frogs

Giant jump
Frogs are superb jumpers

1 The powerful muscles in the frog's hind legs push off

3 The body arches and the front legs act as a brake

2 In mid-leap, the hind legs are fully stretched out and the front legs are held back

Goliath frog

Golden arrow-poison frog

Strawberry poison dart frog

Hamilton's frog

Malaysian horned frog

Toads

Toads spend most of their time on land. They don't have webbed feet and their skin is warty and quite dry

Natterjack toad

These toads hunt for food at night. They can lighten or darken their skin colour to hide from enemies

Common toad

Throat pouch is puffed out when croaking to attract mates

Marine toad

Toxic secretions put off predators

222

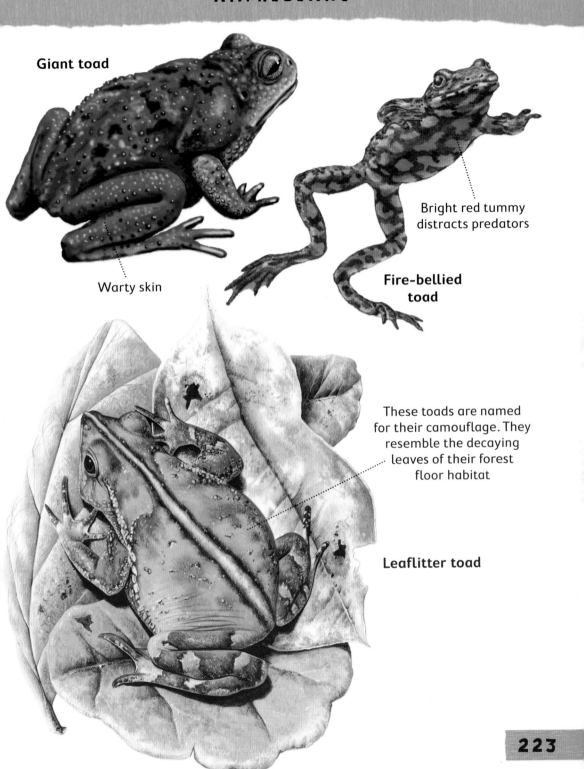

Giant toad

Warty skin

Bright red tummy distracts predators

Fire-bellied toad

These toads are named for their camouflage. They resemble the decaying leaves of their forest floor habitat

Leaflitter toad

Amphibian reproduction

Most amphibians hatch from eggs and grow up in freshwater habitats such as ponds. They move onto land as adults but return to water to breed

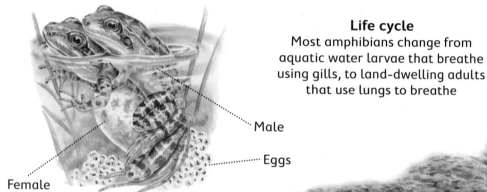

Female

Male

Eggs

Life cycle
Most amphibians change from aquatic water larvae that breathe using gills, to land-dwelling adults that use lungs to breathe

Fertilization
After the female has released her eggs, the male fertilizes them

Key

1 Frogspawn (eggs) float on top of fresh water

2 Tadpoles hatch from the eggs

3 Tadpoles grow legs and change into froglets

4 A froglet loses its tail and grows into an adult frog

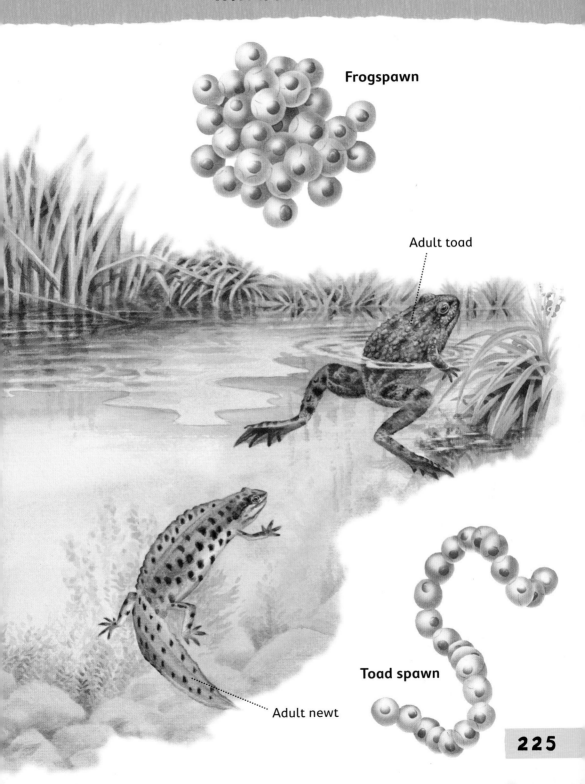

Frogspawn

Adult toad

Adult newt

Toad spawn

Salamanders and newts

These amphibians have slender bodies,
long tails and four legs

Axolotl
These unusual salamanders never
change into the adult form

Feathery
gills

**Mudpuppy
salamander**

**Fire salamander
larva**

Fire salamander

Hellbender salamander

Tiger salamander

Rough-skinned newt

Californian newt

Eastern newt

Moist, slimy skin

Common newt

Great crested newt

Reptiles

This animal group is cold-blooded and mostly lays eggs. Some reptiles live on land while others live in the ocean

Crocodiles and gharials

Crocodiles are large, powerful reptiles with strong bodies, thick skin and snapping jaws. Gharials are smaller members of the crocodile family

Saltwater crocodile
This is the largest type of crocodile. It lives in swamps, rivers and lakes, and also swims out to sea

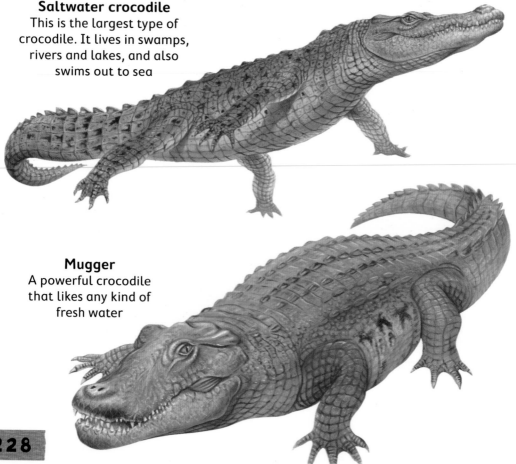

Mugger
A powerful crocodile that likes any kind of fresh water

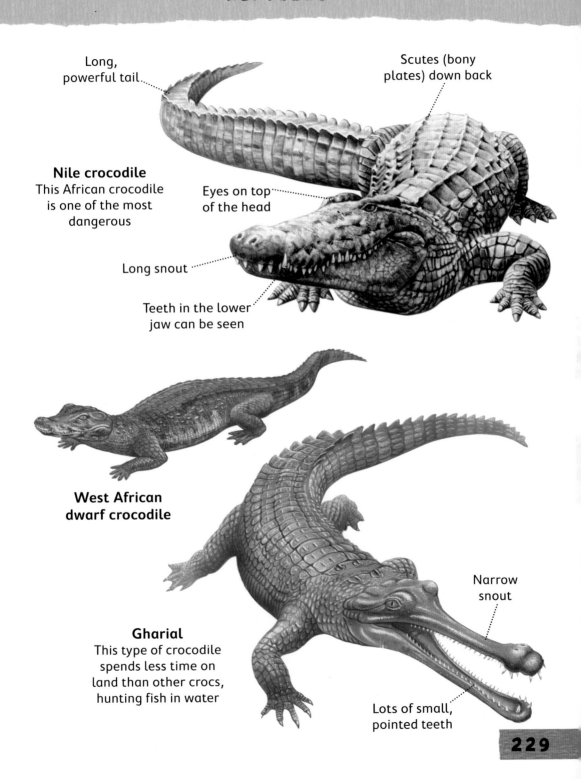

Long, powerful tail

Scutes (bony plates) down back

Nile crocodile
This African crocodile is one of the most dangerous

Eyes on top of the head

Long snout

Teeth in the lower jaw can be seen

West African dwarf crocodile

Gharial
This type of crocodile spends less time on land than other crocs, hunting fish in water

Narrow snout

Lots of small, pointed teeth

229

Alligators and caimans

Alligators are generally smaller than their crocodile
cousins. Caimans are their South American relatives

**American
alligator**

Long,
powerful tail

Scutes (bony plates)
down the back

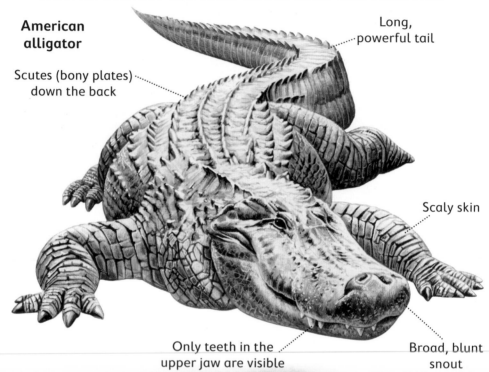

Scaly skin

Only teeth in the
upper jaw are visible

Broad, blunt
snout

**Chinese
alligator**

American alligator and eggs
Alligators are caring mums – they help their babies hatch from their eggs

Common caiman
This reptile eats fish, water birds – even piranhas

Spectacled caiman
The ridge between its eyes gives this reptile its name

Lizards

Scaly-skinned reptiles, lizards live either
on the ground, in rocky areas or in trees

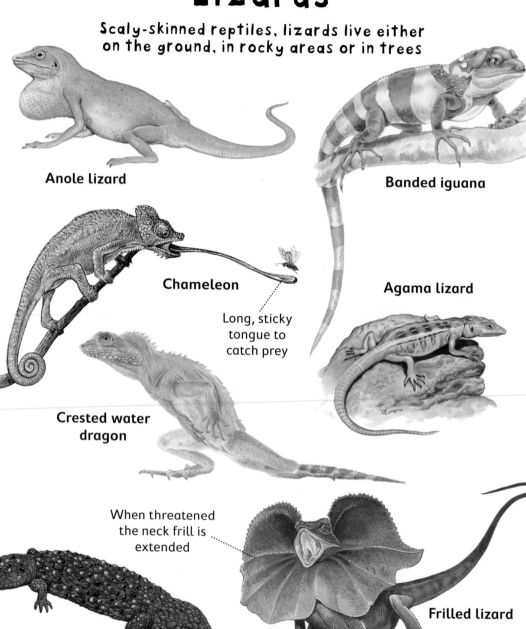

Anole lizard

Banded iguana

Chameleon

Long, sticky
tongue to
catch prey

Agama lizard

Crested water
dragon

When threatened
the neck frill is
extended

Frilled lizard

Shingleback
lizard

232

Komodo dragon

Gecko

Sharp claws

Boyd's forest dragon

Gila monster

Common lizard

Six-lined racerunner

Chuckwalla lizard

233

Venomous snakes

Around **700** species of snake use poison
to immobilize or kill their prey

Boomslang

Adder

King cobra

Hood spread
wide

Puff adder

Leaf-nosed
snake

Yellow-bellied
sea snake

Common
krait

Taipan

Vine
snake

235

Constricting snakes

These snakes squeeze their prey to death by wrapping their strong coils around it

1 The snake holds its prey in its teeth and squeezes it to death in its strong coils

Milk snake

2 When the animal is dead, the snake opens its mouth very wide and starts to swallow its meal

3 The prey forms a bulge in the middle of the snake's body while it is being digested. It may take days, or even weeks, to be fully digested

236

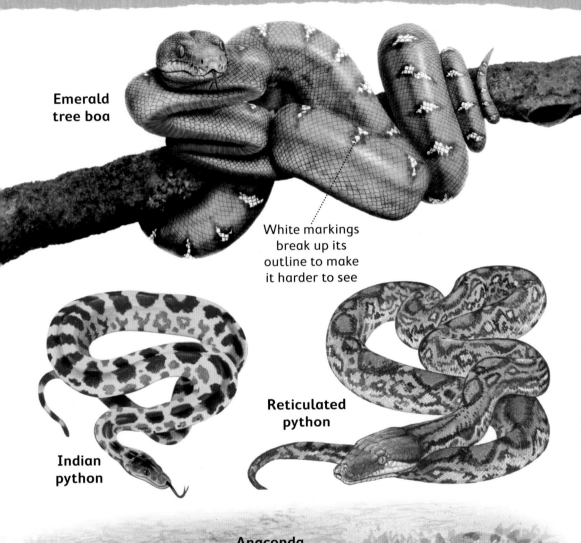

Emerald tree boa

White markings break up its outline to make it harder to see

Indian python

Reticulated python

Anaconda

Snake anatomy

These legless reptiles have long, slender, muscular bodies and are superb hunters

Anatomy

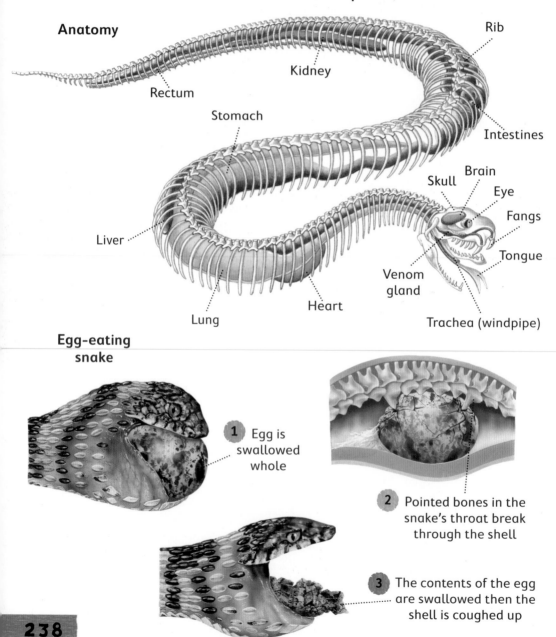

Rib

Kidney

Rectum

Stomach

Intestines

Brain

Skull

Eye

Fangs

Tongue

Liver

Venom gland

Trachea (windpipe)

Heart

Lung

Egg-eating snake

1 Egg is swallowed whole

2 Pointed bones in the snake's throat break through the shell

3 The contents of the egg are swallowed then the shell is coughed up

238

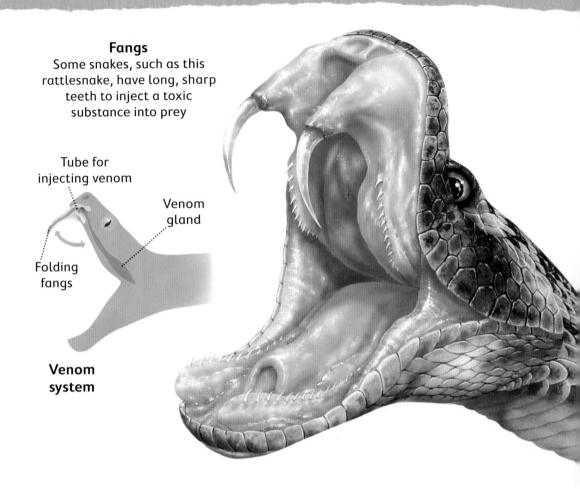

Fangs
Some snakes, such as this rattlesnake, have long, sharp teeth to inject a toxic substance into prey

Tube for injecting venom

Venom gland

Folding fangs

Venom system

Fang position

Primitive snakes
Heavy skulls with a short lower jaw and few teeth

Rear-fanged snakes
Fangs are positioned in the roof of their mouths

Front-fanged snakes
Fangs are positioned at the front of their mouths

Land turtles

These land-living reptiles have toothless beaks and hard, domed shells that are difficult for predators to bite or crush

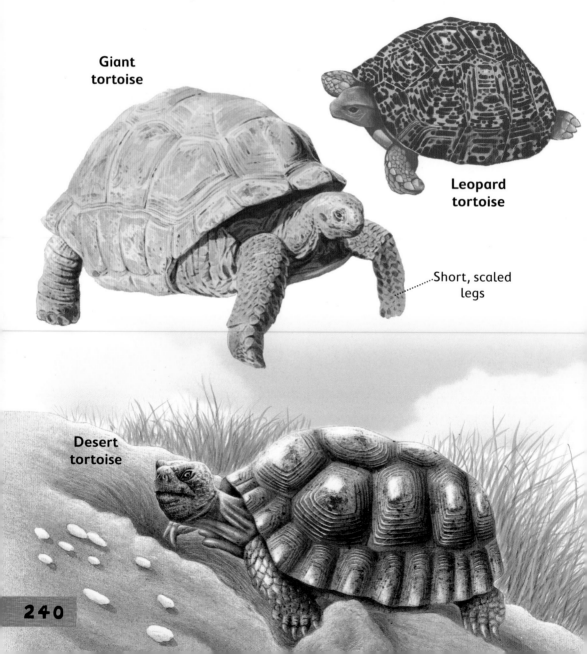

Giant tortoise

Leopard tortoise

......Short, scaled legs

Desert tortoise

**Galapagos
tortoise**

Anatomy

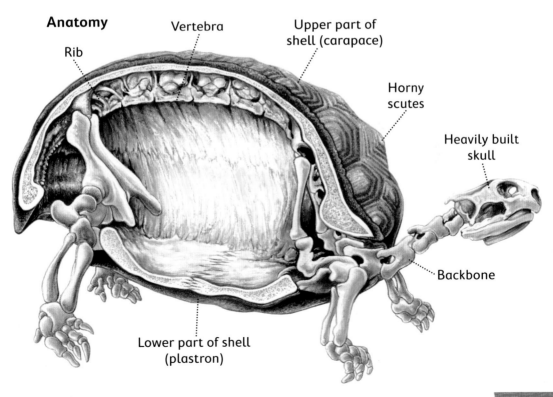

Rib

Vertebra

Upper part of
shell (carapace)

Horny
scutes

Heavily built
skull

Backbone

Lower part of shell
(plastron)

Marine and freshwater turtles

These reptiles have flatter, more streamlined shells. They spend most of their time in water

Snapping turtle

Indian soft shell turtle

Leatherback turtle

Mata mata turtle

Loggerhead turtle hatchlings
Turtle hatchlings must make their way quickly to the safety of the water

242

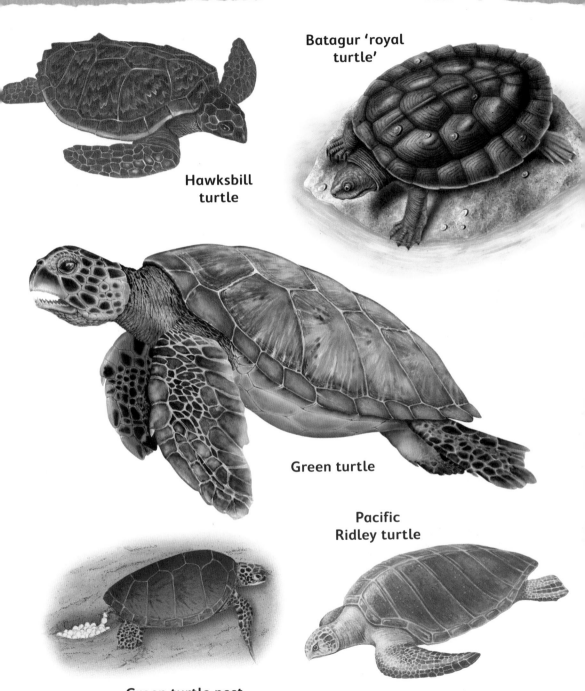

Batagur 'royal
turtle'

Hawksbill
turtle

Green turtle

Pacific
Ridley turtle

Green turtle nest
Females return to the beach where
they hatched to dig their nests

243

Birds

These animals are warm-blooded and have backbones.
Their feathers keep them warm and help some types to
fly. They walk on two back legs, while their front limbs
are wings. All types lay eggs

Bird anatomy

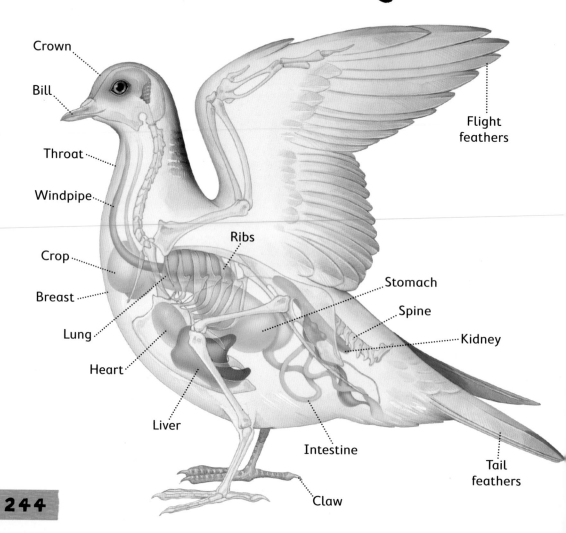

Crown

Bill

Throat

Windpipe

Crop

Breast

Lung

Heart

Liver

Ribs

Stomach

Spine

Kidney

Flight
feathers

Intestine

Tail
feathers

Claw

BIRDS

Feet and talons
Depending on the species, birds have different feet and claw adaptions

Pheasant

Two toes point forwards and two point backwards

Woodpecker

Claws for clinging to tree trunks

Robin

Three forward-pointing toes and one backward-pointing toe

Osprey

Sharp, curved talons to catch prey

Duck

Webs between toes to help with swimming

Nictitating membrane
Some birds, such as this barking owl, have a clear third eyelid

Membrane moves across eye to keep it clean and to protect it from injury

Feathers and flight

Feathers keep birds warm and protect from wind and rain.
The wing and tail feathers allow most birds to fly

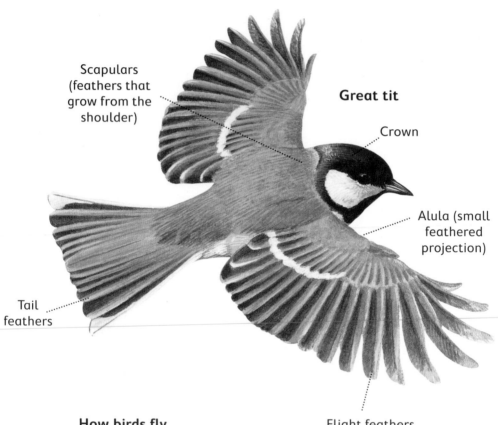

Scapulars (feathers that grow from the shoulder)

Great tit

Crown

Alula (small feathered projection)

Tail feathers

Flight feathers

How birds fly
In flight, a bird's flapping wings make circular up-and-down movements

Types of feather

Soft and
fluffy

Down feather
Traps warm air
next to the body

Tail feather
Used to control
flight

Shape helps to lift
the bird in the air as
well as twist and
turn in flight

Contour
Covers the body,
making it streamlined

Flight feather
These give a continuous
surface area to push the
bird through the air

Nests, eggs and chicks

Most birds make nests in which to lay their eggs and keep them safe, but not all nests are the same

Cave swiftlet

Nest made of feathers and grass, stuck together with the bird's saliva

Weaver bird

1 The male weaver bird twists strips of leaves around a twig

2 Then he makes the roof and the entrance

3 When he's finished, the long entrance helps to provide a safe shelter for the eggs

Mallee fowl
This bird makes a nest of plants covered with sand

Bald eagle
Makes the biggest nest of any bird

Egg varieties

Jacana	Hedge sparrow	Cetti's warbler	Quail	Blue jay
Common snipe	Auk	Scarlet tanager	Catbird	House wren

Peregrine falcon chick

1 A peregrine falcon chick hatches from its egg

2 At two days old, the chick is fluffy and cheeps for food

3 When it is 28 days old, the young bird is growing its adult feathers (plumage) and the old down is falling out

4 Juvenile (young) peregrines have brown feathers, and the face markings are paler than in older birds

Perching birds

There are more than **5700** species of perching birds.
They are small land birds that usually eat mainly seeds,
fruit, nectar and insects

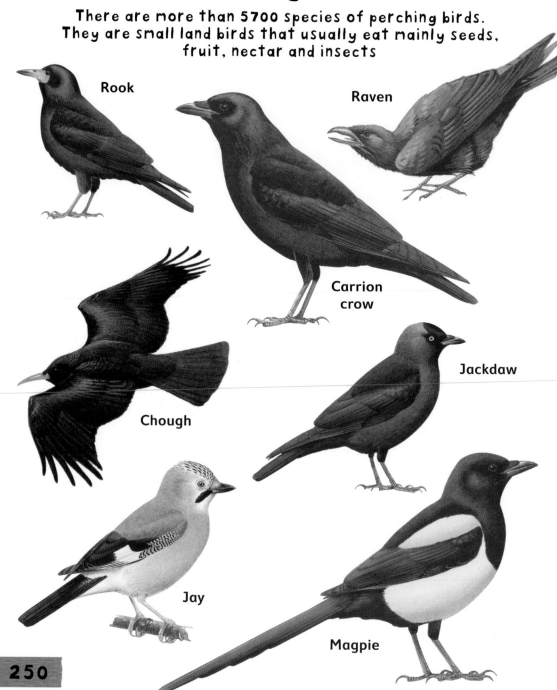

Rook

Raven

Carrion
crow

Chough

Jackdaw

Jay

Magpie

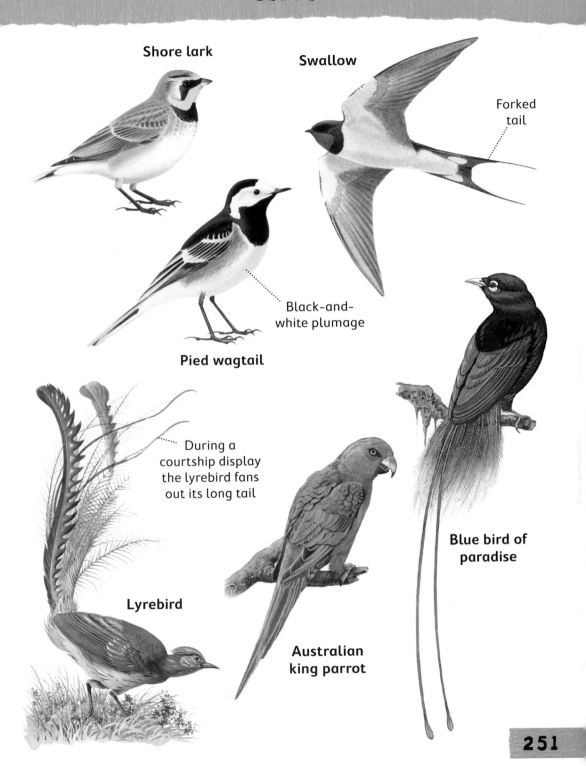

Shore lark

Swallow

Forked
tail

Black-and-
white plumage

Pied wagtail

During a
courtship display
the lyrebird fans
out its long tail

Blue bird of
paradise

Lyrebird

Australian
king parrot

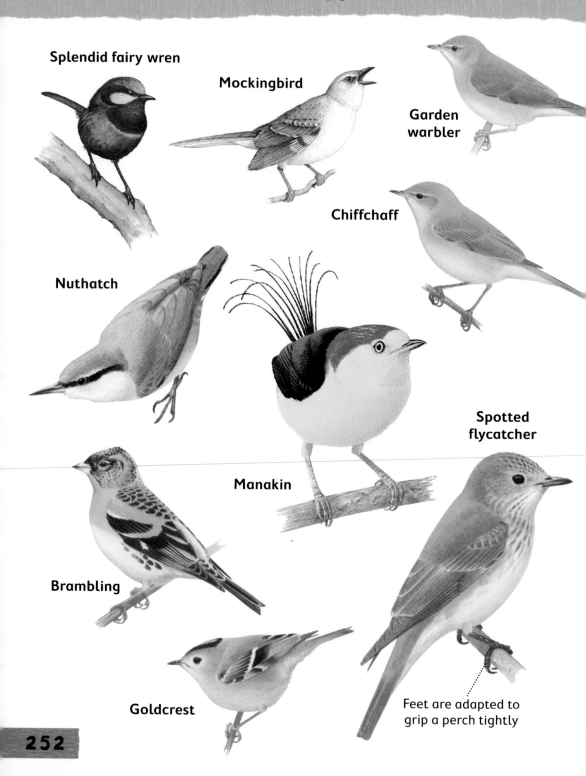

Splendid fairy wren

Mockingbird

Garden
warbler

Chiffchaff

Nuthatch

Spotted
flycatcher

Manakin

Brambling

Goldcrest

Feet are adapted to
grip a perch tightly

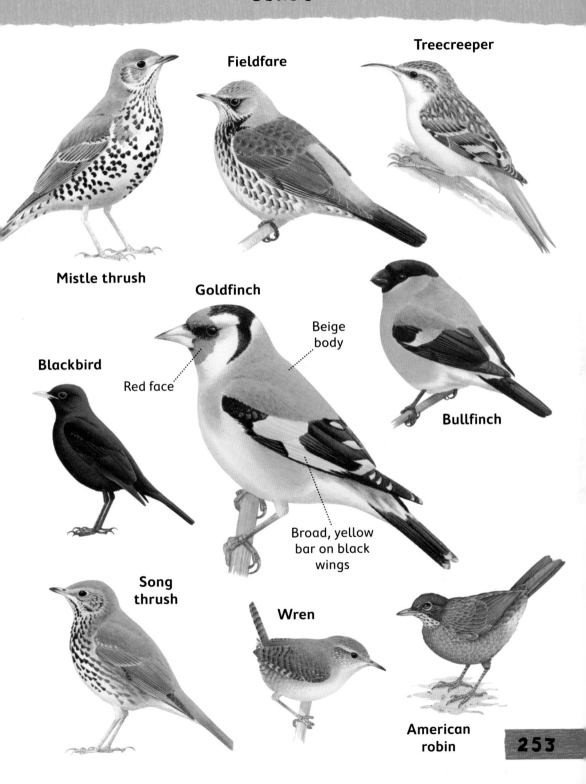

Fieldfare

Treecreeper

Mistle thrush

Goldfinch

Beige body

Blackbird

Red face

Bullfinch

Broad, yellow bar on black wings

Song thrush

Wren

American robin

253

Woodland and forest birds

These birds all live in woodland and forest habitats (homes)

White dove

Jacamar

Feral pigeon

Trogons

Rock dove

254

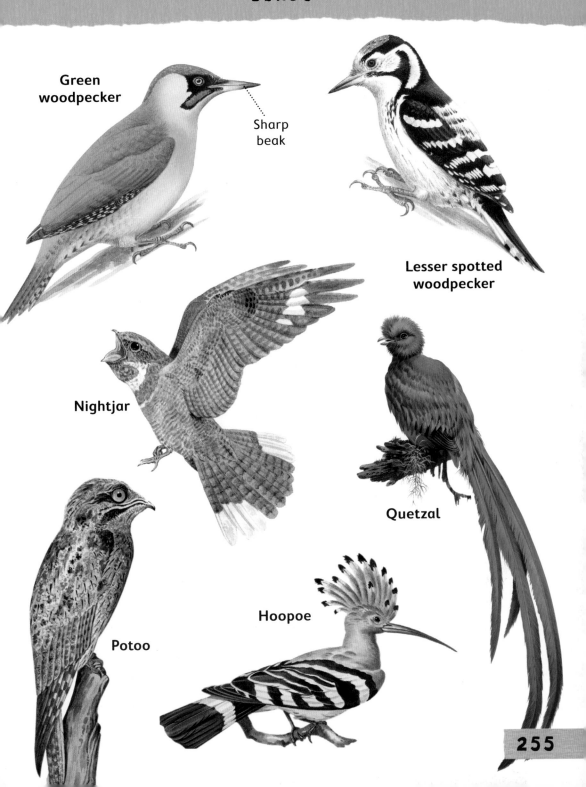

Green
woodpecker

Sharp
beak

Lesser spotted
woodpecker

Nightjar

Quetzal

Potoo

Hoopoe

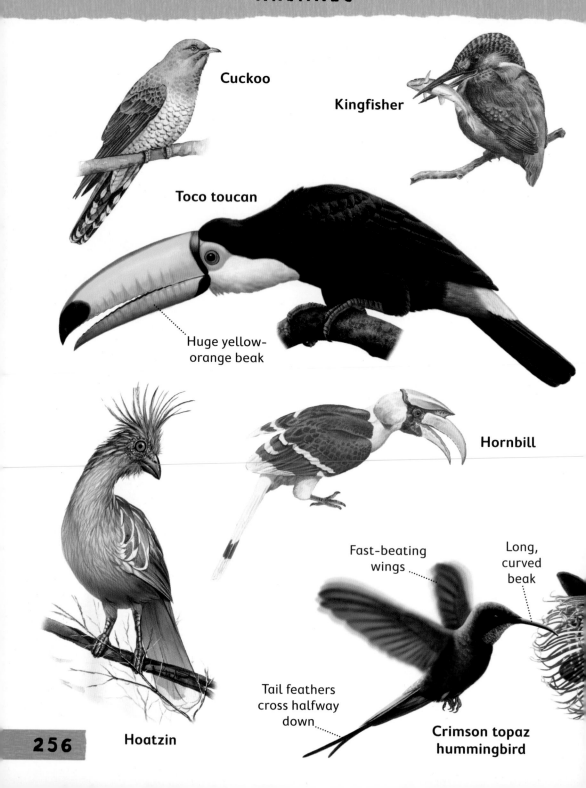

Cuckoo

Kingfisher

Toco toucan

Huge yellow-
orange beak

Hornbill

Fast-beating
wings

Long,
curved
beak

Tail feathers
cross halfway
down

Crimson topaz
hummingbird

Hoatzin

256

Game birds

These birds are mostly large and plump-bodied.
They spend much of their time on the ground and
are often hunted for their meat

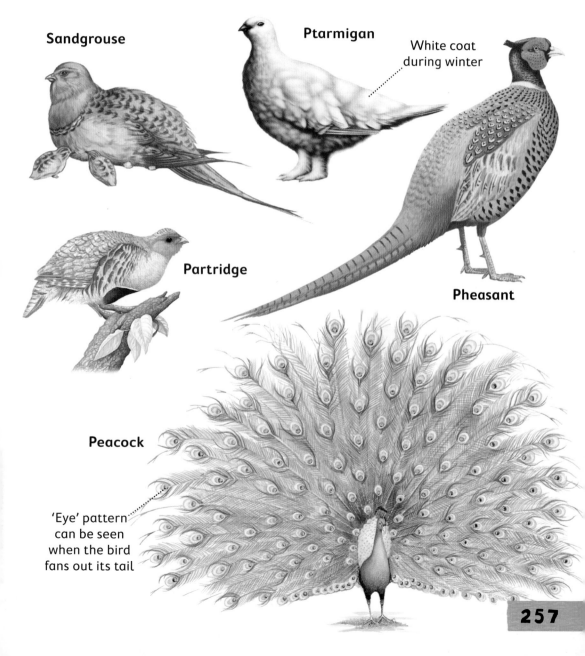

Sandgrouse

Ptarmigan

White coat
during winter

Partridge

Pheasant

Peacock

'Eye' pattern
can be seen
when the bird
fans out its tail

Flightless birds

A small number of birds have lost the ability
to fly – some swim or run to avoid danger

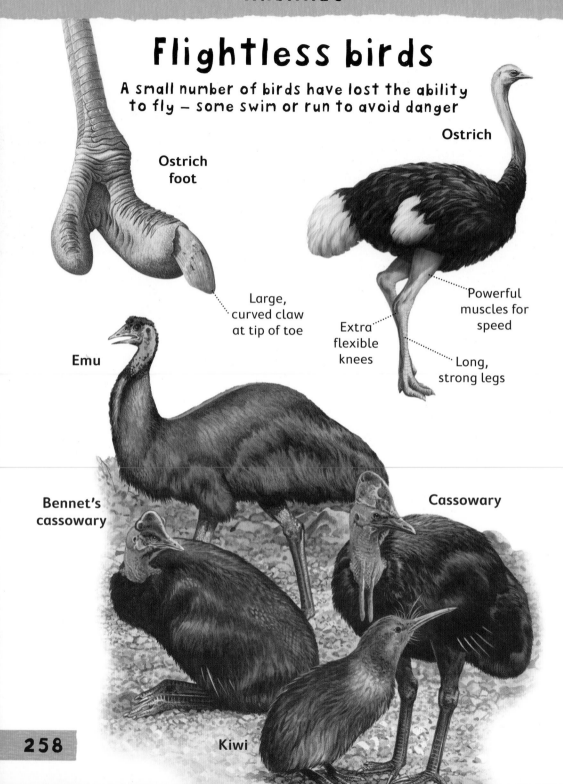

Ostrich
foot

Ostrich

Large,
curved claw
at tip of toe

Powerful
muscles for
speed

Extra
flexible
knees

Long,
strong legs

Emu

Bennet's
cassowary

Cassowary

Kiwi

Rhea

Kakapo
A nocturnal, ground-
dwelling parrot

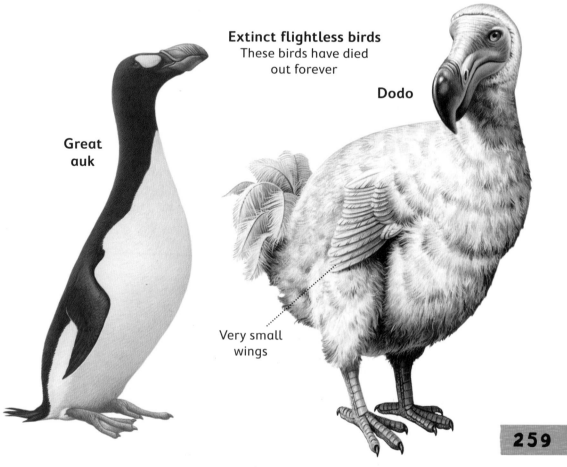

Extinct flightless birds
These birds have died
out forever

Dodo

**Great
auk**

Very small
wings

Waders

These birds often probe wet sand, mud
or grass to find small animals to eat

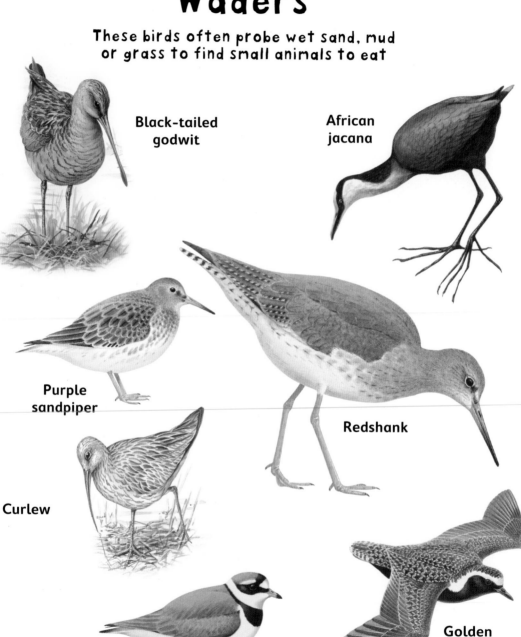

Black-tailed
godwit

African
jacana

Purple
sandpiper

Redshank

Curlew

Ringed
plover

Golden
plover

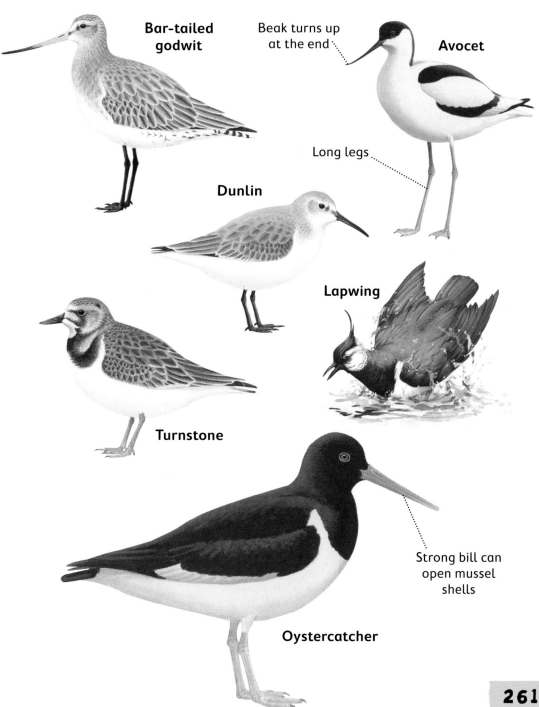

Bar-tailed godwit

Beak turns up at the end :

Avocet

Long legs

Dunlin

Lapwing

Turnstone

Strong bill can open mussel shells

Oystercatcher

Water birds

Water birds live near shallow water
on coasts, lakes, meadows, marshes
and other wetlands all over the world

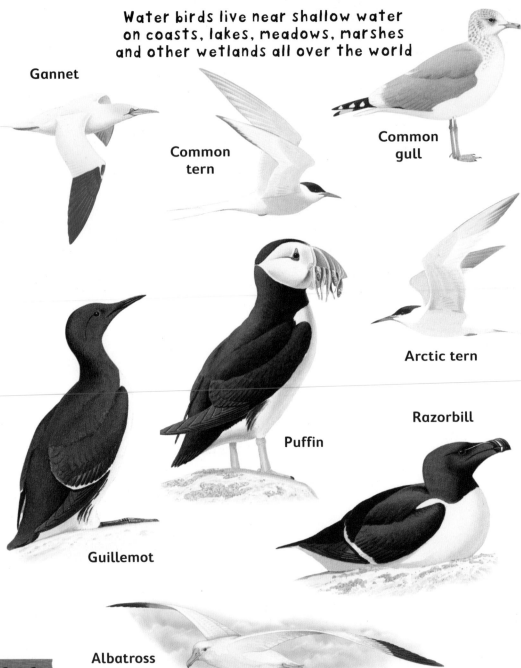

Gannet

Common
tern

Common
gull

Arctic tern

Puffin

Razorbill

Guillemot

Albatross

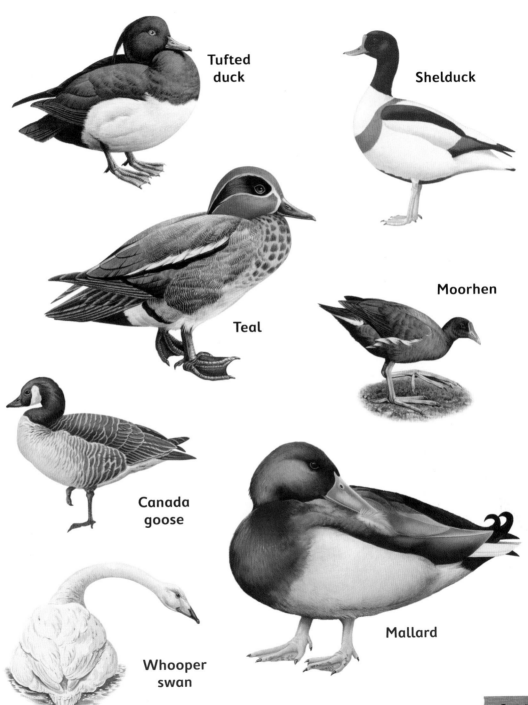

Tufted
duck

Shelduck

Teal

Moorhen

Canada
goose

Mallard

Whooper
swan

Penguins

These flightless water birds have feathers that are more like fur, and wings that are more like flippers

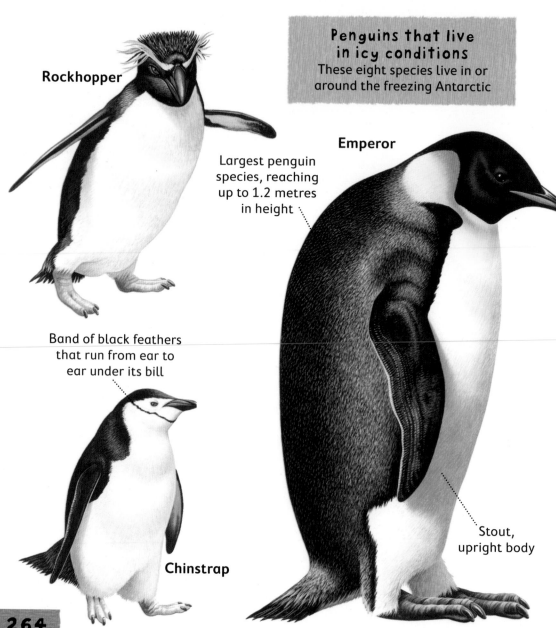

Rockhopper

Penguins that live in icy conditions
These eight species live in or around the freezing Antarctic

Emperor

Largest penguin species, reaching up to 1.2 metres in height

Band of black feathers that run from ear to ear under its bill

Chinstrap

Stout, upright body

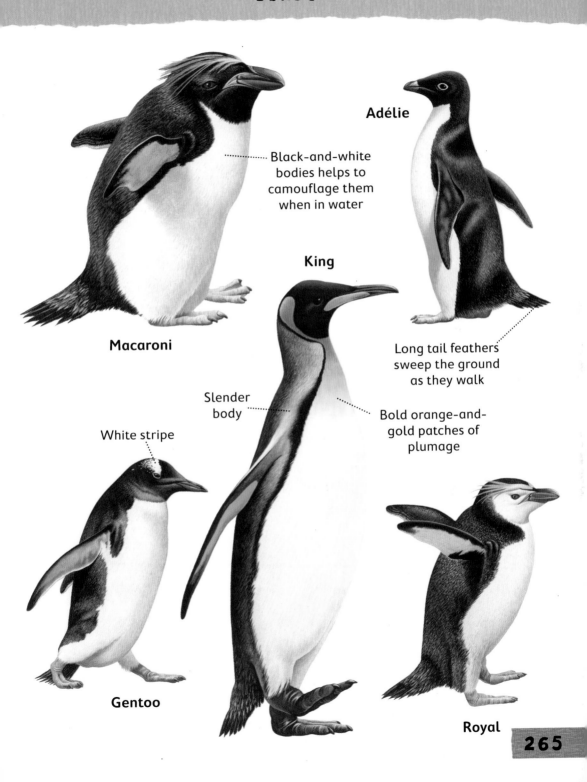

Black-and-white
bodies helps to
camouflage them
when in water

Adélie

King

Long tail feathers
sweep the ground
as they walk

Macaroni

Slender
body

Bold orange-and-
gold patches of
plumage

White stripe

Gentoo

Royal

265

Penguins that live in warm conditions
Found in countries such as South America, Australia, New Zealand and South Africa, and on some islands at the Equator

Peruvian

Black upside-down horseshoe shape on chest

Galapagos

Yellow-eyed

Stiff, flipper-like wings

Snares

Webbed feet

Erect-crested

Fjordland

Yellow feathers above each eye

Little

Smallest penguin species, reaching just 35 centimetres in height

Magellanic

Black dots

Jackass

Birds of prey

A group of hunting birds (raptors) with
sharp talons and bills to seize prey

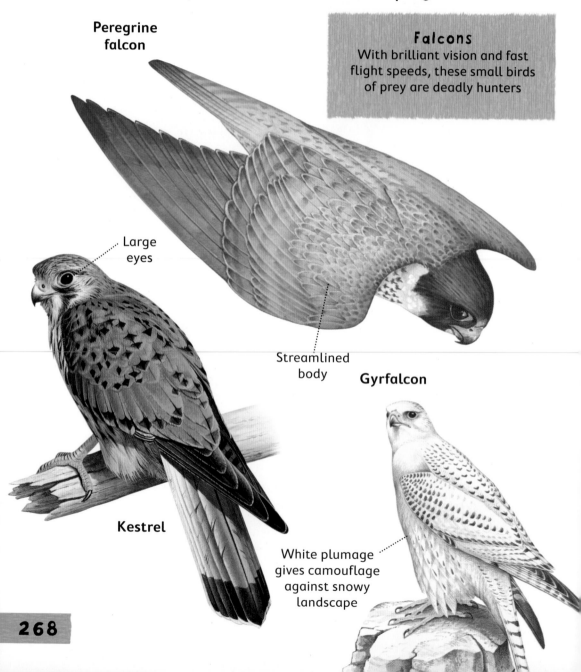

Peregrine falcon

Falcons
With brilliant vision and fast
flight speeds, these small birds
of prey are deadly hunters

Large eyes

Streamlined body

Gyrfalcon

Kestrel

White plumage
gives camouflage
against snowy
landscape

268

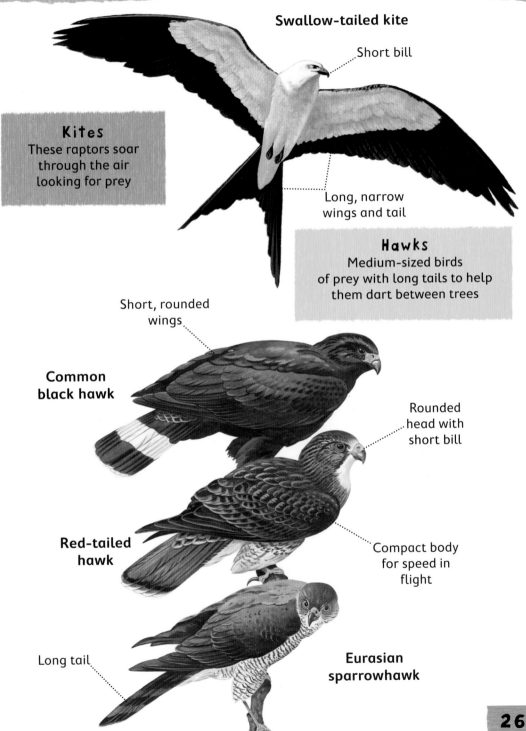

Swallow-tailed kite

Short bill

Kites
These raptors soar
through the air
looking for prey

Long, narrow
wings and tail

Hawks
Medium-sized birds
of prey with long tails to help
them dart between trees

Short, rounded
wings

**Common
black hawk**

Rounded
head with
short bill

**Red-tailed
hawk**

Compact body
for speed in
flight

Long tail

**Eurasian
sparrowhawk**

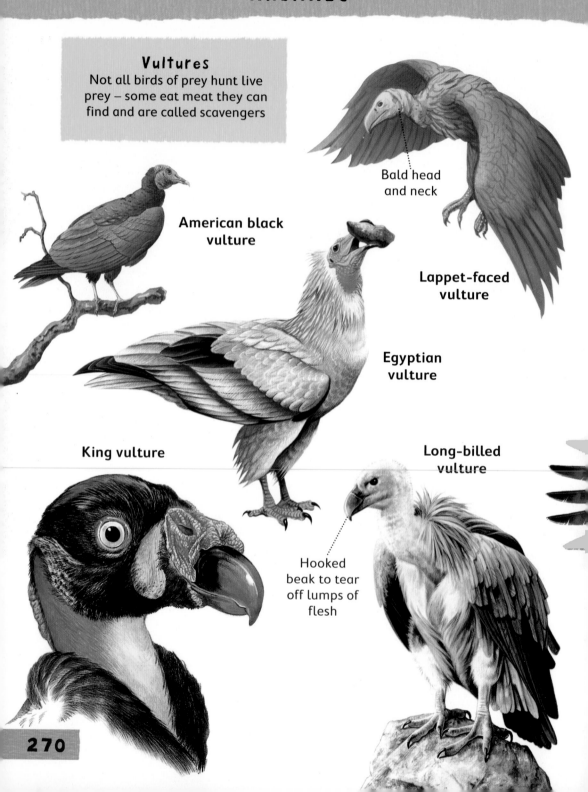

Vultures
Not all birds of prey hunt live prey – some eat meat they can find and are called scavengers

Bald head and neck

American black vulture

Lappet-faced vulture

Egyptian vulture

King vulture

Long-billed vulture

Hooked beak to tear off lumps of flesh

270

Eagles
Large, heavy-bodied birds with strong legs, big bills and feet, and broad wings

Grey head feathers

Golden eagle

Black plumage on back

Harpy eagle

Rusty-brown feathers

Large, heavy bill

White-tailed eagle

Long head feathers

Blue-grey bill

Philippine eagle

Owls

Most owls hunt prey at night. They are equipped with sharp talons and bills, as well as large, forward-facing eyes

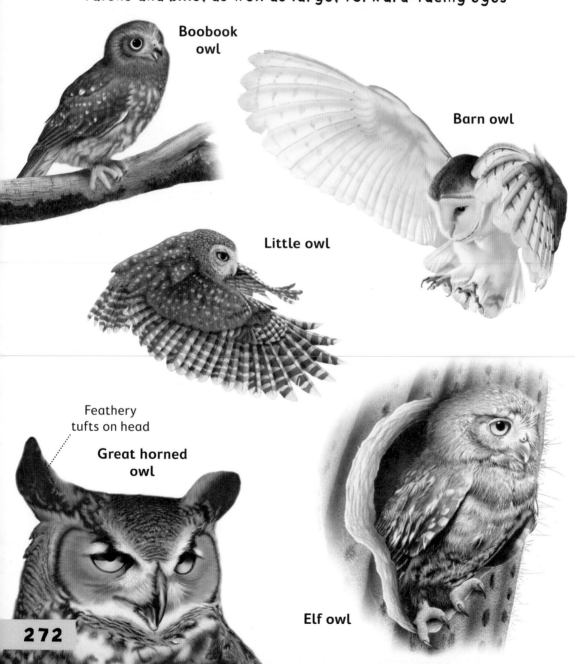

Boobook owl

Barn owl

Little owl

Feathery tufts on head

Great horned owl

Elf owl

272

Tawny owl

Eagle owl

Scops owl

Brown fish owl

Snowy owl

Chick

Mammals

A group of warm-blooded animals with a bony skeleton. Being warm-blooded means that a mammal can keep its body at a constant temperature. The skeleton supports the body and protects the delicate organs inside

Monotremes

The only group of egg-laying mammals

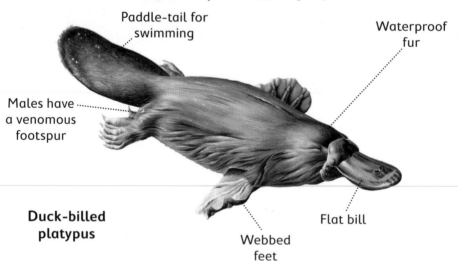

Paddle-tail for swimming

Waterproof fur

Males have a venomous footspur

Duck-billed platypus

Flat bill

Webbed feet

Echidna

Long snout used to sniff out termites, ants, worms and grubs

Egg is kept inside a pouch on the stomach

Spines

274

Marsupials

These unusual mammals give birth to tiny, undeveloped
young that grow inside the mother's pouch

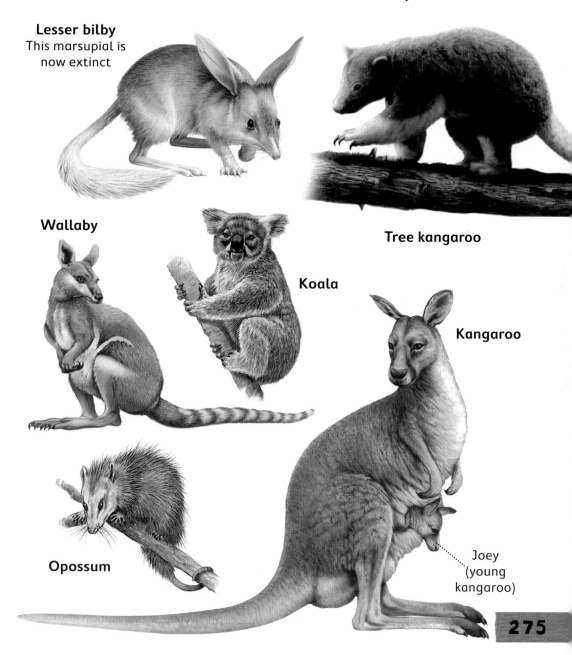

Lesser bilby
This marsupial is
now extinct

Wallaby

Koala

Tree kangaroo

Kangaroo

Opossum

Joey
(young
kangaroo)

275

Bats

These small, furry animals are the only mammals that can fly. They are mostly active at night

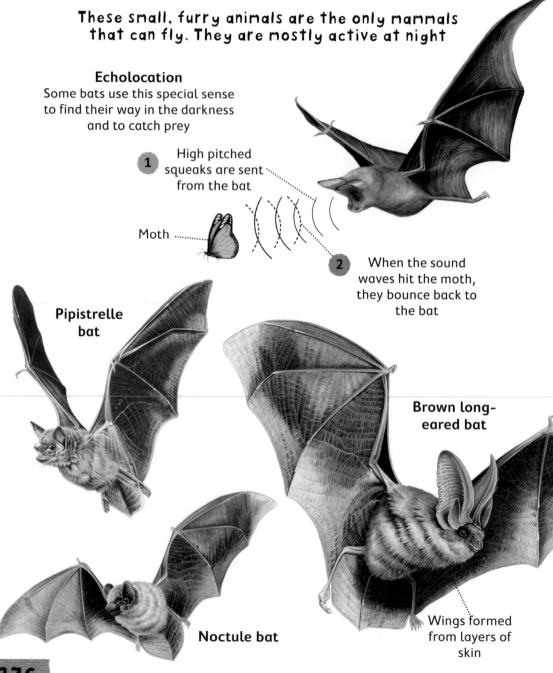

Echolocation
Some bats use this special sense to find their way in the darkness and to catch prey

1 High pitched squeaks are sent from the bat

Moth

2 When the sound waves hit the moth, they bounce back to the bat

Pipistrelle bat

Brown long-eared bat

Noctule bat

Wings formed from layers of skin

276

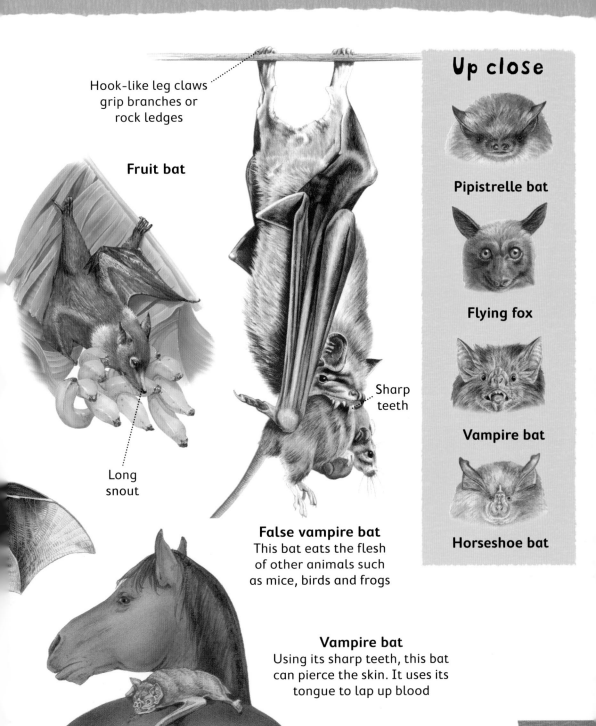

Hook-like leg claws
grip branches or
rock ledges

Fruit bat

Up close

Pipistrelle bat

Flying fox

Long
snout

Sharp
teeth

Vampire bat

Horseshoe bat

False vampire bat
This bat eats the flesh
of other animals such
as mice, birds and frogs

Vampire bat
Using its sharp teeth, this bat
can pierce the skin. It uses its
tongue to lap up blood

Monkeys

Most monkeys live in social groups,
often with one dominant male.
All types have tails

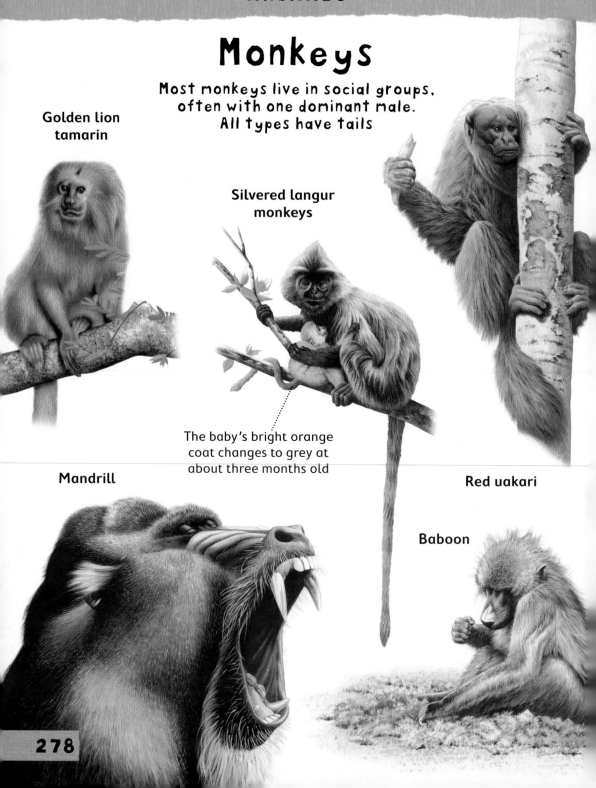

Golden lion tamarin

Silvered langur monkeys

The baby's bright orange
coat changes to grey at
about three months old

Mandrill

Red uakari

Baboon

278

Dark eyebrows and orange crown

De Brazza's monkey

Black-handed spider monkeys

Male

Adults have long, droopy snouts

Female

Baby

Long arms, legs and tails allow this monkey to swing through trees at speed

Proboscis monkeys

Crab-eating macaque

Apes

Apes are intelligent mammals and our closest living relatives. They have front limbs that are longer than the hind limbs, and no tail

Gibbon
These fast-moving apes can swing through trees at great speed

Bonobo

Like chimps, bonobos lean on their knuckles when they walk

Chimpanzees

Chimps insert sticks into termite mounds to catch and eat the insects

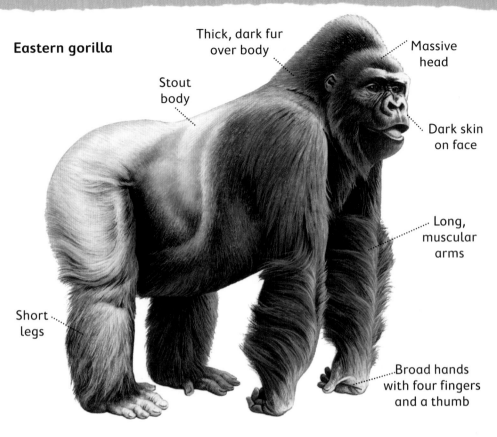

Eastern gorilla

Thick, dark fur over body

Massive head

Stout body

Dark skin on face

Long, muscular arms

Short legs

Broad hands with four fingers and a thumb

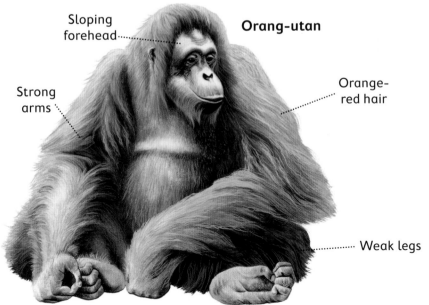

Sloping forehead

Orang-utan

Strong arms

Orange-red hair

Weak legs

281

Prosimians

Related to monkeys and apes, most prosimians
live in trees and can leap from branch
to branch with great accuracy

Large ears
and eyes

Tarsier

**Slender
loris**

Slow loris

**Lesser
bushbaby**

Long tail

282

Aye-aye

Long middle finger used to probe trees for tasty grubs

Ruffed lemur

Banded tail

Ring-tailed lemur

Moles, hedgehogs and shrews

Small mammals also known as 'insectivores', which means 'insect-eaters'

Hedgehog

Mole

Shovel-like paws

Spines protect the body

Water shrew

Long, pointed, whiskery nose

Cuban solenodon

Small eyes and ears

Pygmy shrew

Rabbits and hares

These animals live in open, grassy country and have long ears, large eyes and twitching noses

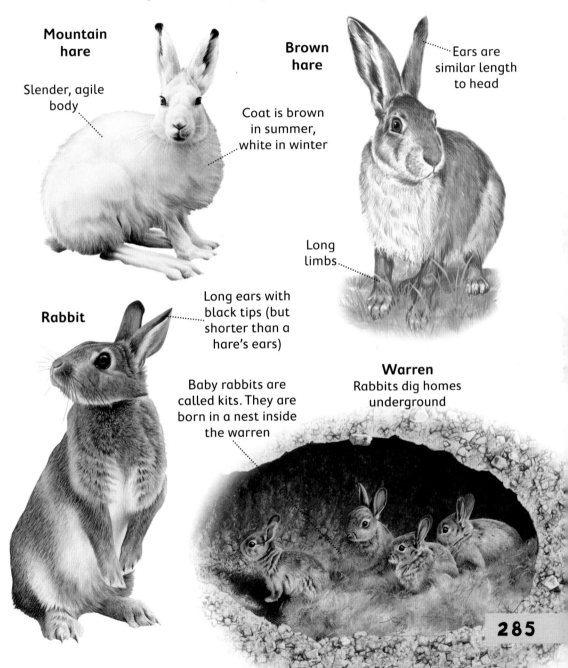

Mountain hare

Slender, agile body

Coat is brown in summer, white in winter

Brown hare

Ears are similar length to head

Long limbs

Rabbit

Long ears with black tips (but shorter than a hare's ears)

Baby rabbits are called kits. They are born in a nest inside the warren

Warren
Rabbits dig homes underground

Rodents

Rodents are usually small, four-legged
creatures with long tails and sharp senses

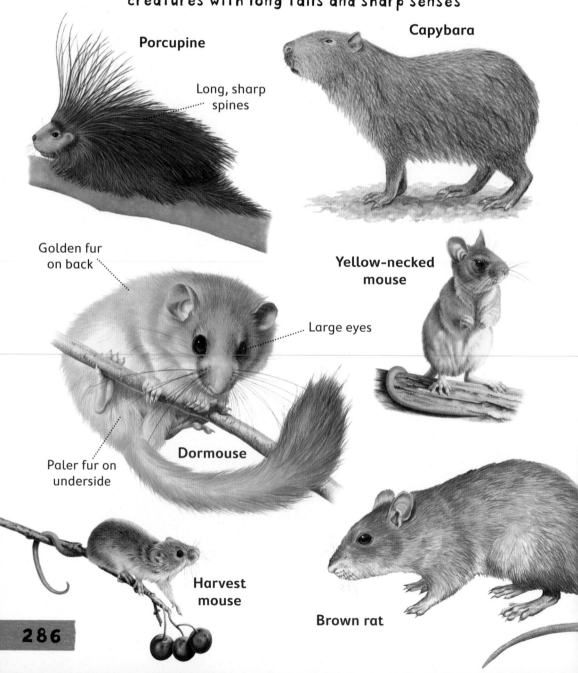

Porcupine

Long, sharp
spines

Capybara

Golden fur
on back

**Yellow-necked
mouse**

Large eyes

Paler fur on
underside

Dormouse

Harvest
mouse

Brown rat

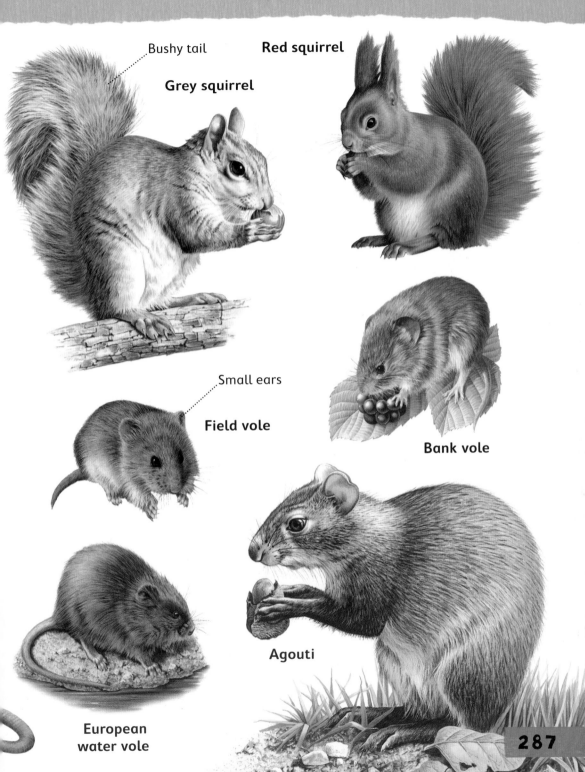

Bushy tail

Red squirrel

Grey squirrel

Small ears

Field vole

Bank vole

Agouti

European water vole

Whales

Whales belong to the family of mammals known as 'cetacea'.
They spend all their lives in the ocean, breathe air, give birth
to live young and feed their babies with milk

Sperm whale
Chasing a giant
squid

Huge, square
head

Fluke

Small eye

**Beluga whale
and calf**

Long, straight
tusk

**Blue whale
and calf**

Narwhals

Grey whale
and calf

Calf stays close
to its mother

Barnacles
stuck to skin

Bowhead
whale

Humpback whale

289

Dolphins and porpoises

Superb swimmers that belong to the same family as whales

Common dolphin

Triangular dorsal fin

Dark-grey to black upper body

Elongated beak

Long flippers

Flukes pointed at tips, with central notch

Sides light-grey to yellow

Dark circles around the eyes, with a dark line running between them

Striped dolphin and calf

Spectacled porpoise

Atlantic spotted
dolphin

Bottlenose
dolphin

Killer whale

Harbour
porpoise

Dall's
porpoise

Finless
porpoise

291

Wild dogs

Dogs that aren't tame and live in the wild are found almost everywhere, yet many species are endangered

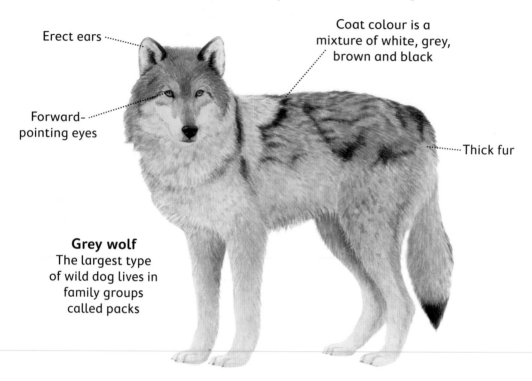

Erect ears ·········

Coat colour is a mixture of white, grey, brown and black

Forward-pointing eyes ·········

·········Thick fur

Grey wolf
The largest type of wild dog lives in family groups called packs

Grey fox

Jackal

Coyote

Dingo

Black fur
on ears

Red fox

Long, thick
tail, known as
a 'brush'

Reddish-
brown fur

Domestic dogs

All tame dogs are descended from wolves. For thousands of years, people have bred dogs to develop types (breeds) with particular characteristics

Hounds
These dogs have been developed for hunting. Some hunt using sight while others use their sense of smell

Bloodhound

Irish Wolfhound

Beagle

Basset Hound

Dachshund

Whippet

Gundogs
Gundogs were developed to follow hunters, find prey and retrieve birds or other animals that had been shot

English Cocker Spaniel

Blue eyes

Weimaraner

Long legs

Grey-brown coat

Strong body

Labrador Retriever

Working dogs
These dogs are usually obedient and energetic. They are intelligent, so can be easily trained

Saint Bernard

Boxer

German Shepherd

295

Terriers

These small dogs were bred to chase small wild animals, such as rabbits. They are clever, active dogs

Parson Jack Russell

Border Terrier

Scottish Terrier

Staffordshire Bull Terrier

Toy dogs

Toy dogs tend to be very small. They have been bred to be family pets and companions

Pug

Bichon Frise

Chihuahua

296

Shar Pei

Ears are set high on the head

Spotted coat

Dalmatian

Long tail has an upward curve

Strong, square body

Short, neat coat

Round paws

Bulldog

Schnauzer

Dog anatomy

Wild dogs and domestic dogs all belong to a family
called canids. Canids are intelligent animals with long,
lean bodies, slender legs and bushy tails

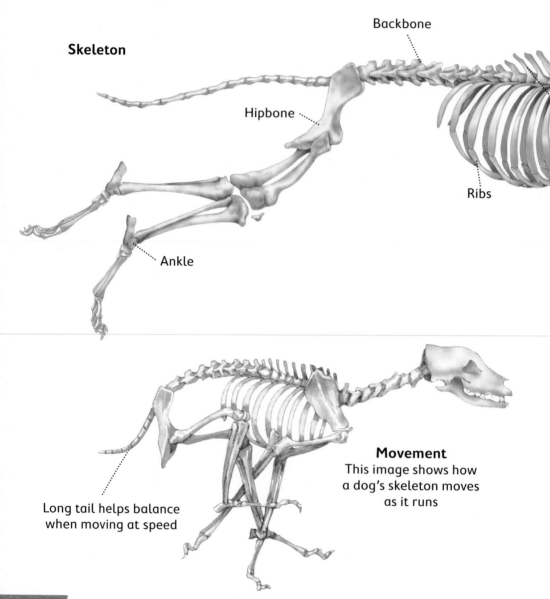

Skeleton

Backbone

Hipbone

Ribs

Ankle

Movement
This image shows how
a dog's skeleton moves
as it runs

Long tail helps balance
when moving at speed

Ears
Wolves' ears are large, upright and pointed, but modern domestic dogs have ears in a variety of shapes and sizes

Skull

Shoulder blade

Grey wolf

Great Dane

Paw

Claws cannot be retracted (pulled back into paw)

Irish Terrier

Pug

Bears

All bears have large, heavy bodies, big heads and short, powerful legs

Black ears

Round, white face with black rings around the eyes

Giant panda and cub

Spectacled bear

American black bear

Black limbs and white body

Asian black bear

300

Stocky body

Thick, shaggy, fur

Sun bear

Large front paws with claws

Polar bear

Sloth bear and cubs

Brown bear

Mustelids

A group of short-legged, sharp-toothed hunters.
Most types have long tails and long, slender bodies

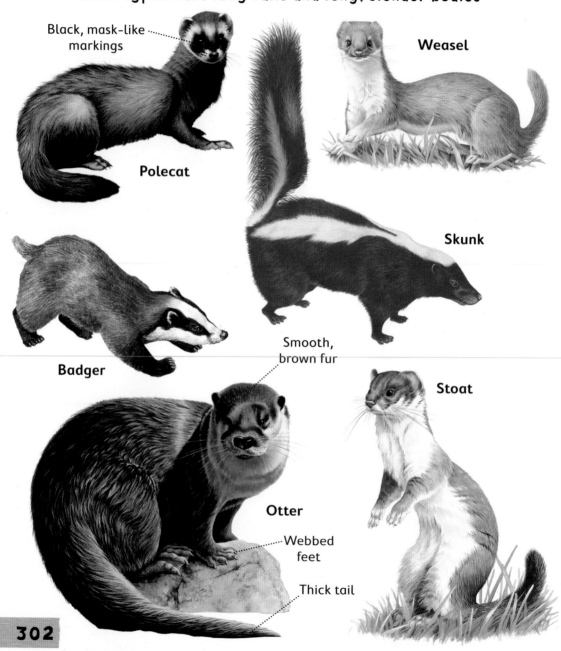

Black, mask-like
markings

Weasel

Polecat

Skunk

Badger

Smooth,
brown fur

Stoat

Otter

Webbed
feet

Thick tail

302

Mongooses

These small mammals are found mostly in Africa and Asia, where they live in burrows. Mongooses are agile enough to kill snakes such as cobras

Meerkat
A member of the mongoose animal family

Narrow, tapered face with pointed nose

Fingers with claws

Feet with four toes

Cusimanse mongoose

Long, thin tail with black tip

Mongoose attacking a cobra
The mongoose is partly immune to the snake's venom and is protected by its thick fur coat

303

Wild cats

This meat-eating group includes some of the most skilled hunters in the animal kingdom

Jaguar

Lion

Golden-brown coat

Shaggy mane around the head and neck

Lynx

Snow leopard

Red-orange coat with vertical black stripes

Powerful shoulders and thick neck

Tail with black rings

Tiger

Caracal

Puma

Clouded
leopard

Cheetah

Leopard
With gazelle
prey

Domestic cats

These small, tame cats have been bred to develop certain appearances and personalities. Most cats have coats with long or short hair

Shorthaired

British White

Almond-shaped eyes

Thin, dainty body

Siamese

Long, thin legs

Elegant paws

British Black

Snowshoe

Russian Blue

Thick blue coat with silvery sheen

Stripy coat

Tabby

British
Tortoiseshell

Bengal

Burmese

Savannah

Cornish
Rex

British Bi-Colour

ANIMALS

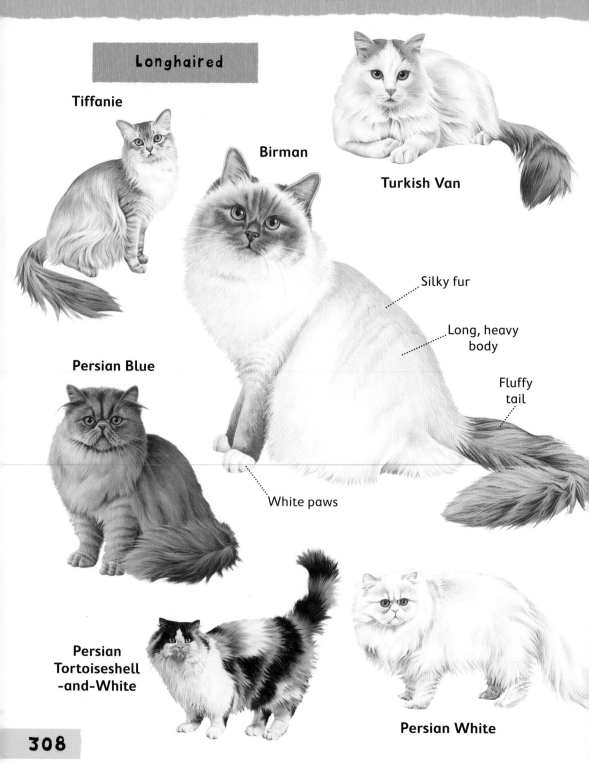

Longhaired

Tiffanie

Birman

Turkish Van

Silky fur

Long, heavy body

Fluffy tail

Persian Blue

White paws

Persian Tortoiseshell -and-White

Persian White

308

MAMMALS

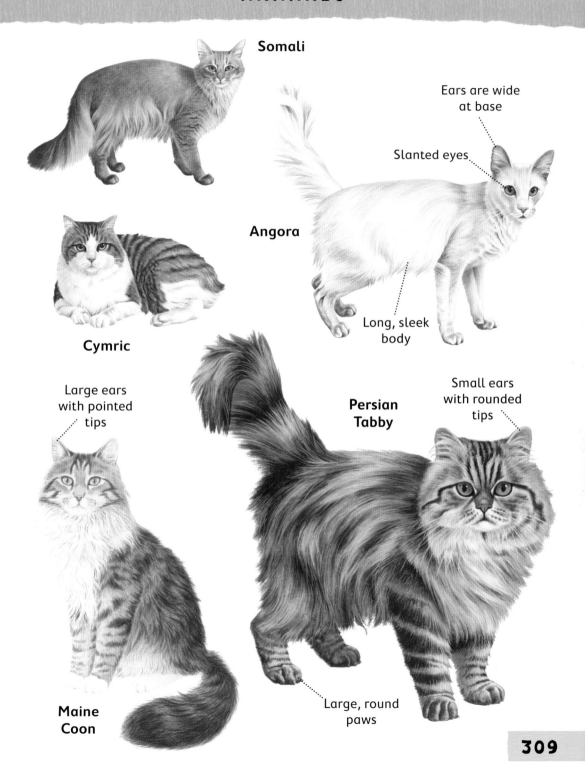

Somali

Ears are wide
at base

Slanted eyes

Angora

Long, sleek
body

Cymric

Large ears
with pointed
tips

Persian
Tabby

Small ears
with rounded
tips

Maine
Coon

Large, round
paws

Cat anatomy

All cats, domestic and wild, belong to a group of
animals called 'felidae'. They have keen senses,
quick reactions and great agility

Skull

**Domestic cat
skeleton**

Backbone

Hip
bone

Shoulder
blade

Ribs

Claw

Toe bone

Long, flexible,
spring-like spine

Small, flat
ribcage aids
breathing

Movement
Cheetahs are the world's fastest
land animals. Their anatomy
allows them to run at great
speeds over short distances

Hip joints swivel on
the spine, giving
longer strides

Large heart
and strong
arteries

Claws

Retracted claws

Non-retracted claws

.... Tail bone

Vision

Pupil closed ....

Bright daylight
The cat's pupil narrows to a slit, allowing less daylight in

Pupil open ....

Darkness
The pupil widens to let in as much light as possible

Rough tongue
Papillae – bumps on the surface of the tongue that help grip food while the teeth are chewing

Nictitating membrane ....

Nictitating membrane
A cat has a 'third eyelid', or nictitating membrane. This can move partly across to protect the eye

Elephants, hippos and rhinos

These mammals are the largest animals on land

African elephant

Asian elephant

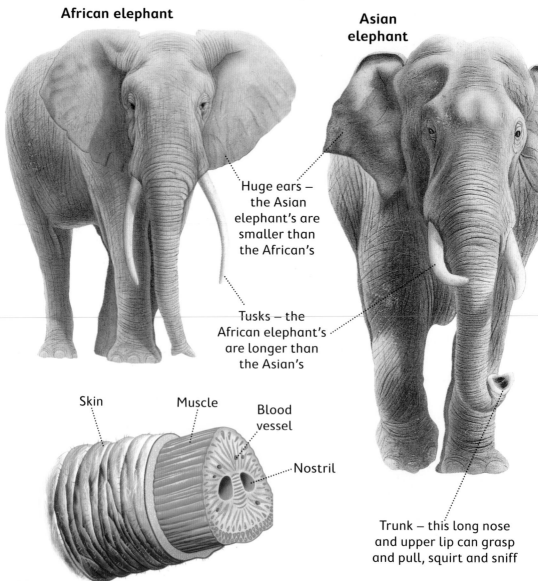

Huge ears — the Asian elephant's are smaller than the African's

Tusks — the African elephant's are longer than the Asian's

Skin

Muscle

Blood vessel

Nostril

Trunk — this long nose and upper lip can grasp and pull, squirt and sniff

Inside a trunk

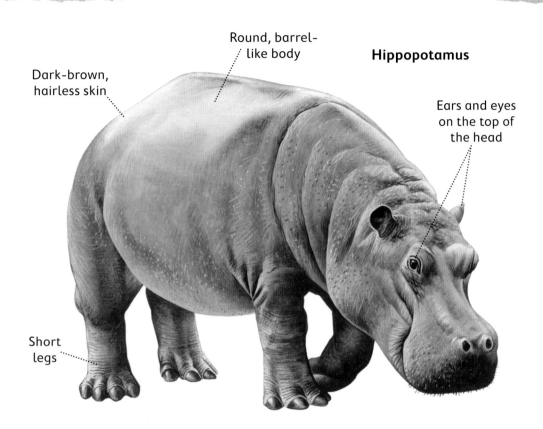

Round, barrel-like body

Dark-brown, hairless skin

Hippopotamus

Ears and eyes on the top of the head

Short legs

White rhino

Sharp horn

Sumatran rhino

Indian rhino

Javan rhino

Black rhino

Hoofed mammals

Some mammals have hoofed feet. Most have
one or two hooves on each foot

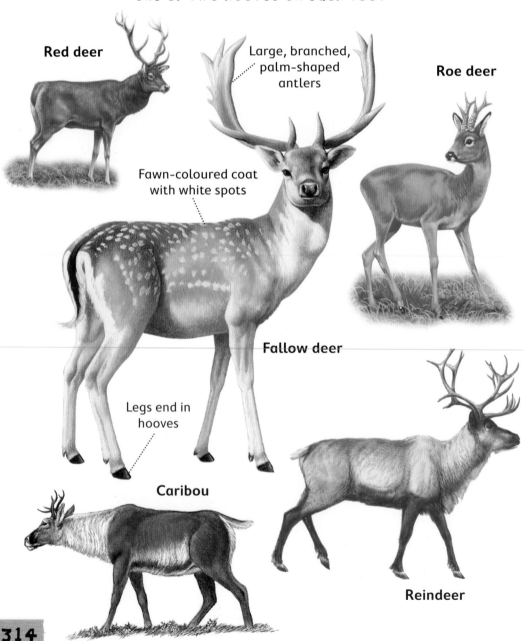

Red deer

Large, branched,
palm-shaped
antlers

Roe deer

Fawn-coloured coat
with white spots

Fallow deer

Legs end in
hooves

Caribou

Reindeer

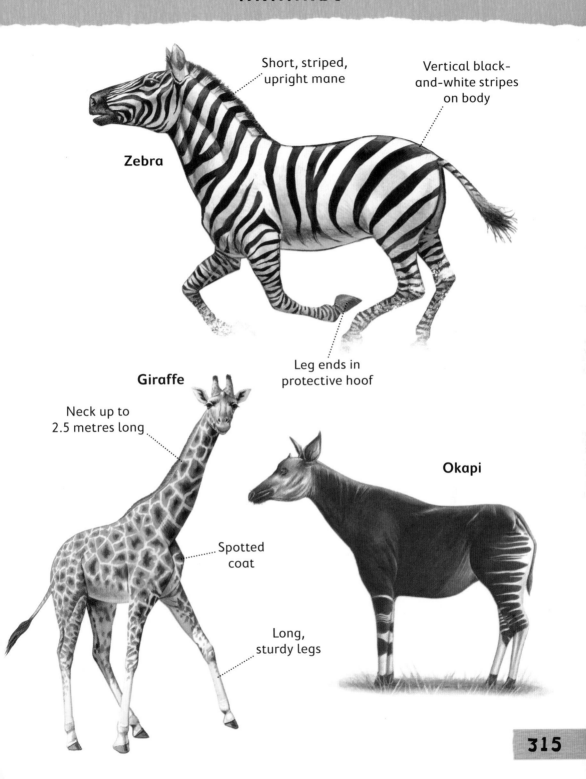

Short, striped, upright mane

Vertical black-and-white stripes on body

Zebra

Leg ends in protective hoof

Giraffe

Neck up to 2.5 metres long

Okapi

Spotted coat

Long, sturdy legs

Horses

The three types of horse are hotbloods (elegant and fast), coldbloods (large, heavy and strong) and warmbloods (developed by breeding hotbloods with coldbloods)

Wide body

Suffolk
Coldblood

Quarter horse
Warmblood

Appaloosa
Warmblood

316

Camargue
Warmblood

Przewalski's horse
A true wild horse that
has never been tamed

Strong,
muscular
body

Shire
Coldblood

Lipizzaner
Warmblood

Arab
Hotblood

Horse anatomy

Skeleton

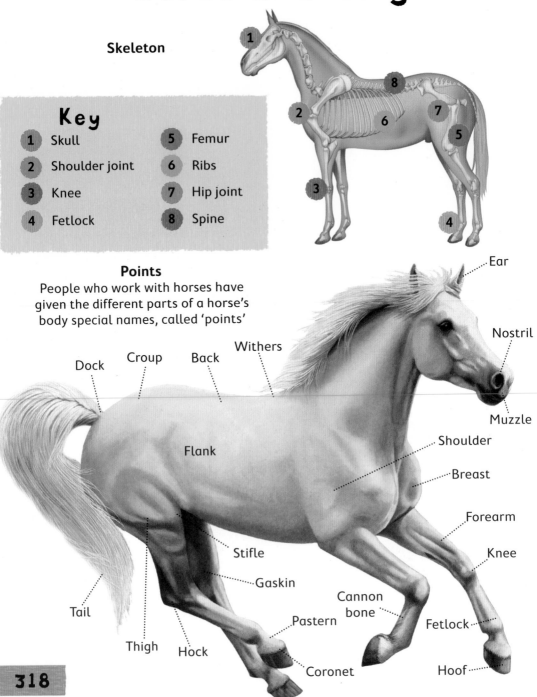

Key

1	Skull	**5**	Femur
2	Shoulder joint	**6**	Ribs
3	Knee	**7**	Hip joint
4	Fetlock	**8**	Spine

Points
People who work with horses have given the different parts of a horse's body special names, called 'points'

Dock
Croup
Back
Withers
Ear
Nostril
Muzzle
Flank
Shoulder
Breast
Forearm
Knee
Stifle
Gaskin
Tail
Cannon bone
Pastern
Fetlock
Thigh
Hock
Coronet
Hoof

MAMMALS

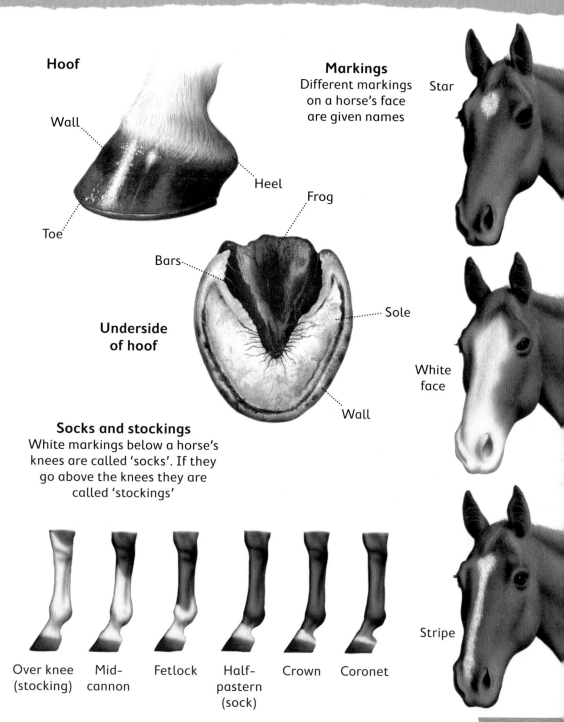

Hoof

Wall

Heel

Toe

Underside of hoof

Bars

Frog

Sole

Wall

Markings
Different markings on a horse's face are given names

Star

White face

Stripe

Socks and stockings
White markings below a horse's knees are called 'socks'. If they go above the knees they are called 'stockings'

Over knee (stocking)

Mid-cannon

Fetlock

Half-pastern (sock)

Crown

Coronet

Ponies

Usually smaller than horses, ponies have wider bodies and shorter legs. They are hardy animals and can live in extreme environments

Welsh cob pony

White, or pale yellow mane

Fell pony

Haflinger mare (female) and foal

MAMMALS

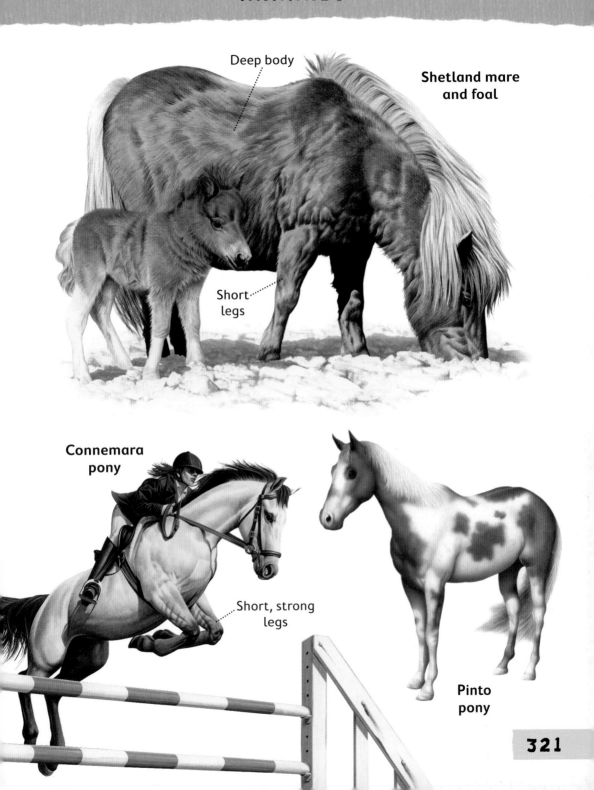

Deep body

Shetland mare and foal

Short legs

Connemara pony

Short, strong legs

Pinto pony

Rib cage
This hard casing of bone protects vital organs such as the heart and lungs

HUMAN BODY

Cells

Cells are the tiny, basic building blocks of your body.
In your body there are over 200 different kinds of cell,
including bone cells, blood cells and muscle cells

Key

1   Cell membrane
A thin layer of protein
and fat surrounds the cell

2   Mitochondria
These release energy by
breaking down sugars in
the blood

3   Nucleus
The cell's control centre

4   Golgi bodies
These send chemicals to
parts of the body where
they are needed

5   Cytoplasm
A jelly-like liquid that
fills the cell

6   Lysosomes
These are the cell's rubbish
bins. They digest any
unwanted material

Internal view
This diagram shows the
layers and parts of a
single cell

DNA

Inside every cell there is a substance called DNA. It carries all your genes. These are the body's chemical instructions and hold information for growth, survival and having children

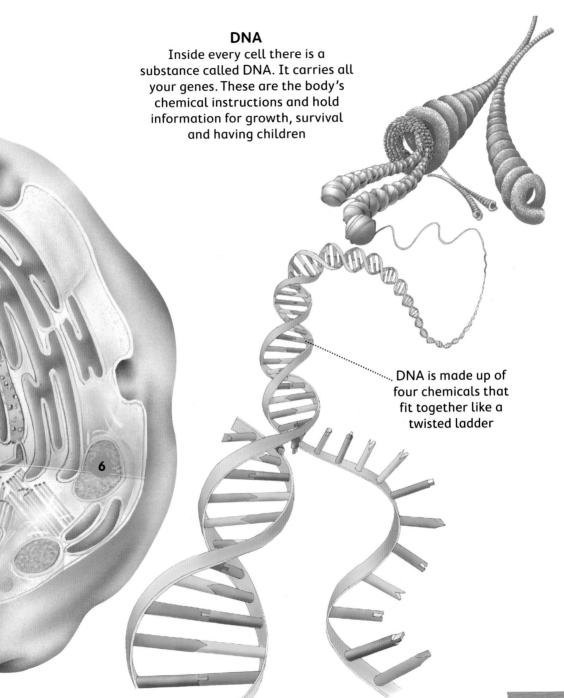

DNA is made up of four chemicals that fit together like a twisted ladder

6

Circulatory System

Blood is transported around the body by a network of vessels

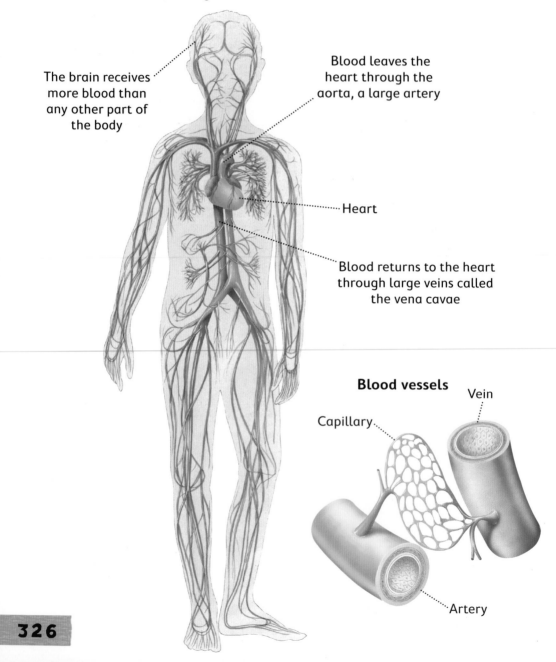

The brain receives more blood than any other part of the body

Blood leaves the heart through the aorta, a large artery

Heart

Blood returns to the heart through large veins called the vena cavae

Blood vessels

Vein

Capillary

Artery

Inside a blood vessel

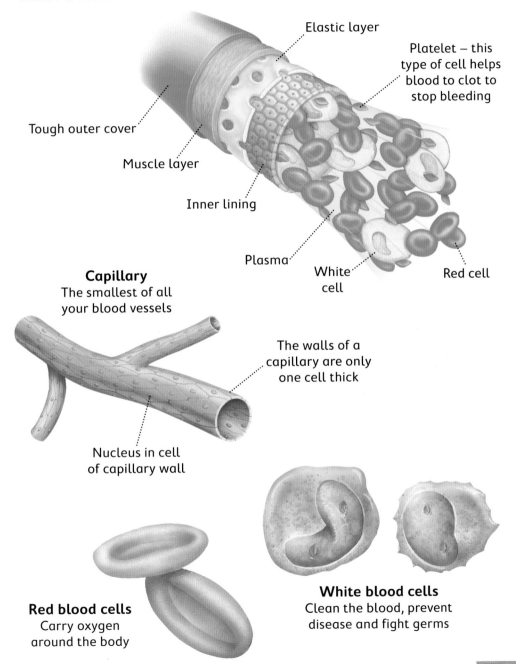

Elastic layer

Platelet – this type of cell helps blood to clot to stop bleeding

Tough outer cover

Muscle layer

Inner lining

Plasma

White cell

Red cell

Capillary
The smallest of all your blood vessels

The walls of a capillary are only one cell thick

Nucleus in cell of capillary wall

Red blood cells
Carry oxygen around the body

White blood cells
Clean the blood, prevent disease and fight germs

Heart

A pump made almost entirely of muscle. The stronger left ventricle (lower chamber) pumps blood around the body, and the smaller right ventricle pumps blood to the lungs

Superior vena cava brings blood from the upper body into the right atrium

Internal view

Aorta sends blood rich in oxygen around the body

Pulmonary artery takes blood to the lungs to pick up oxygen

Pulmonary veins bring blood back from the lungs and into the left atrium, ready to be pumped around the body

Left atrium

Right atrium

Left ventricle

Right ventricle

Location

Inferior vena cava brings blood from the lower body

Heartbeat

The heart squeezes and expands to pump blood containing oxygen around the body

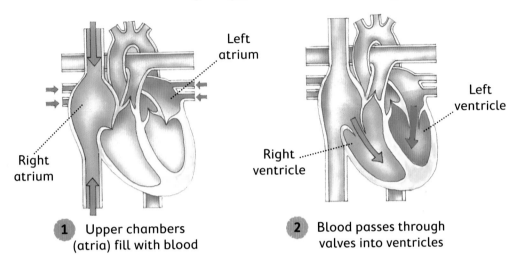

Left atrium

Right atrium

1 Upper chambers (atria) fill with blood

Left ventricle

Right ventricle

2 Blood passes through valves into ventricles

3 The ventricles contract, pushing blood into the arteries

Blood goes to lungs to pick up oxygen

4 Blood starts to fill up the relaxed atria from the veins

Blood with oxygen being pumped around the body

Respiratory system

The lungs, airways and diaphragm make up this breathing system

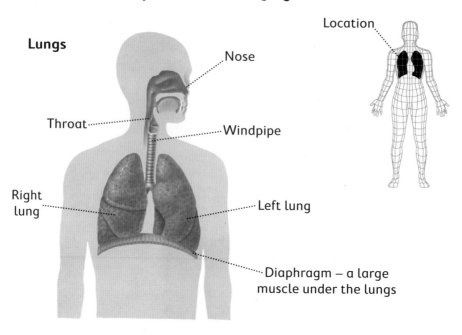

Lungs

Nose

Throat

Windpipe

Right lung

Left lung

Diaphragm – a large muscle under the lungs

Location

Breathing in

Air in

Diaphragm pulls down

Breathing out

Air out

Diaphragm relaxes

Lungs

The lungs inside your chest consist of bunches of tiny air sacs called 'alveoli', which transfer oxygen to the blood and pick up carbon dioxide from the blood

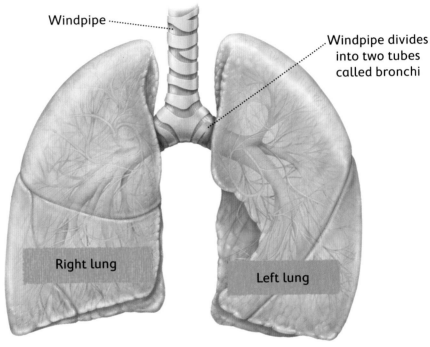

Windpipe

Windpipe divides into two tubes called bronchi

Right lung

Left lung

Inside the bronchi

Muscles in wall

Air space

Bronchiole

Alveoli

Air space

Alveoli
The bronchi divide into smaller bronchioles. At the end of each one is a group of tiny air sacs called alveoli

331

Digestive system

Breaks down food so it can be absorbed by the body

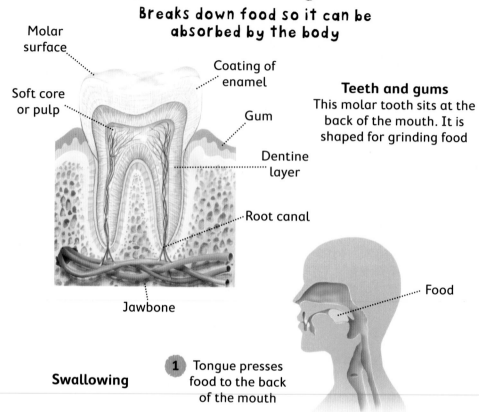

Molar surface

Coating of enamel

Soft core or pulp

Gum

Teeth and gums
This molar tooth sits at the back of the mouth. It is shaped for grinding food

Dentine layer

Root canal

Jawbone

Food

Swallowing

1 Tongue presses food to the back of the mouth

2 Food passes over the top of the windpipe

3 Food is pushed down the gullet, through the chest and into the stomach

Gullet (oesophagus)

Windpipe

Chest

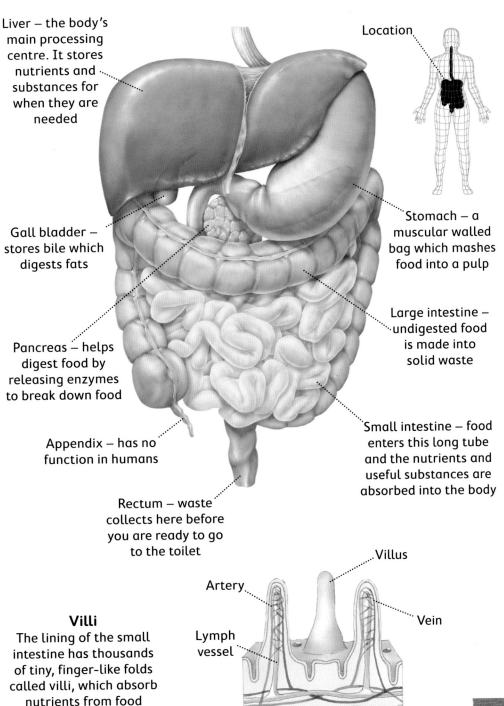

Liver – the body's main processing centre. It stores nutrients and substances for when they are needed

Location

Gall bladder – stores bile which digests fats

Stomach – a muscular walled bag which mashes food into a pulp

Pancreas – helps digest food by releasing enzymes to break down food

Large intestine – undigested food is made into solid waste

Appendix – has no function in humans

Small intestine – food enters this long tube and the nutrients and useful substances are absorbed into the body

Rectum – waste collects here before you are ready to go to the toilet

Villus

Artery

Vein

Lymph vessel

Villi
The lining of the small intestine has thousands of tiny, finger-like folds called villi, which absorb nutrients from food

Urinary system

Removes waste products from the blood and the body

Location

Kidney — filters the blood to produce urine

Ureter (connects kidney to bladder)

Bladder

Reproductive system

The organs that enable people to reproduce (have babies)

Female reproductive system

Key

1 Ovary – where egg cells are stored

2 Fallopian tube – egg cells travel along this tube and into the uterus

3 Uterus – can stretch to fit a baby as it grows in the womb

4 Cervix – entrance to the womb

5 Vagina – the canal from the uterus to the outside of the body

Male reproductive system

Key

1 Urethra

2 Penis

3 Testes – where sperm cells are made

Sperm cell

Head

Tail

Nucleus

Baby development

The growth of a baby inside its mother's womb

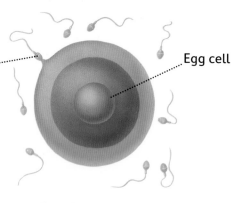

Sperm cell about to fertilize egg cell

Egg cell

Fertilization
A single sperm cell fertilizes the female egg cell

Pregnancy

8 weeks
Main organs are formed

12 weeks
Heart beats, and kicking movements begin

16 weeks
Face has taken shape and bones of skeleton start to form

Placenta (food and oxygen are passed to the baby via the placenta)

20 weeks
Hair begins to grow

32 weeks
Fat collects under skin

Umbilical cord (runs between the baby and the placenta)

Cervix (neck of womb)

36 weeks
Baby usually turns head down

40 weeks
Ready for birth

Skeleton

Supports the body, protects major organs
and provides an anchor for the muscles

Cranium
(skull)

Mandible (jaw)

Sternum
(breastbone)

Clavicle
(collarbone)

Scapula
(shoulder blade)

Humerus

Rib

Radius

Vertebra
(backbone)

Ulna

Femur
(thigh bone)

Pelvis (hip bone)

Patella
(kneecap)

Tibia

Fibula

Bones and joints

The skeleton is made up of bones. Joints hold bones together and allow them to move

Inside a bone

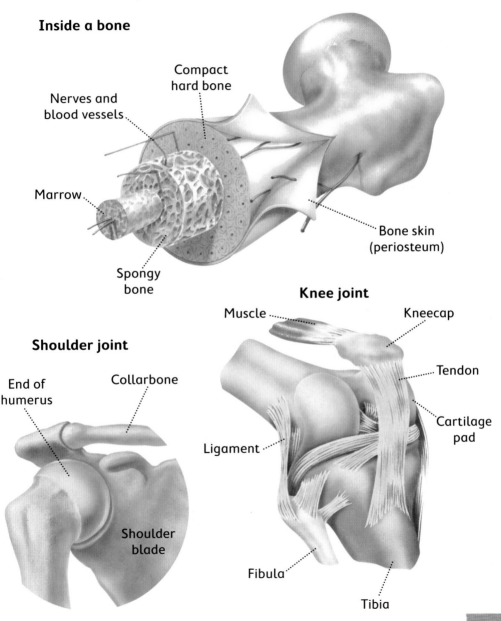

Compact hard bone

Nerves and blood vessels

Marrow

Spongy bone

Bone skin (periosteum)

Knee joint

Muscle

Kneecap

Tendon

Cartilage pad

Ligament

Shoulder joint

End of humerus

Collarbone

Shoulder blade

Fibula

Tibia

339

Muscles

Special fibres that contract (tighten) and relax to move parts of the body

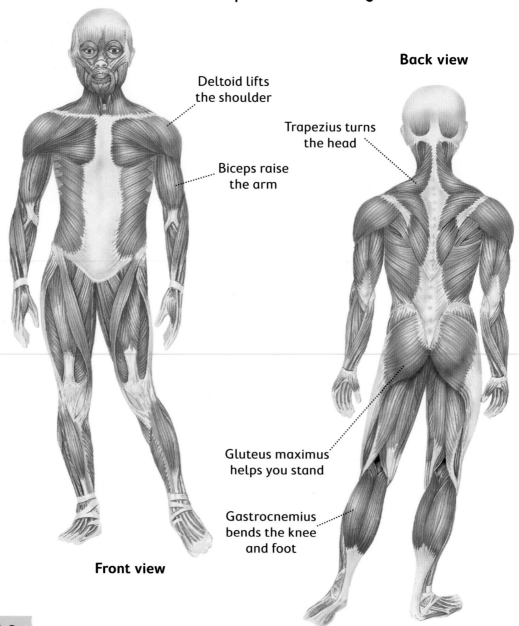

Back view

Deltoid lifts
the shoulder

Trapezius turns
the head

Biceps raise
the arm

Gluteus maximus
helps you stand

Gastrocnemius
bends the knee
and foot

Front view

Inside a muscle

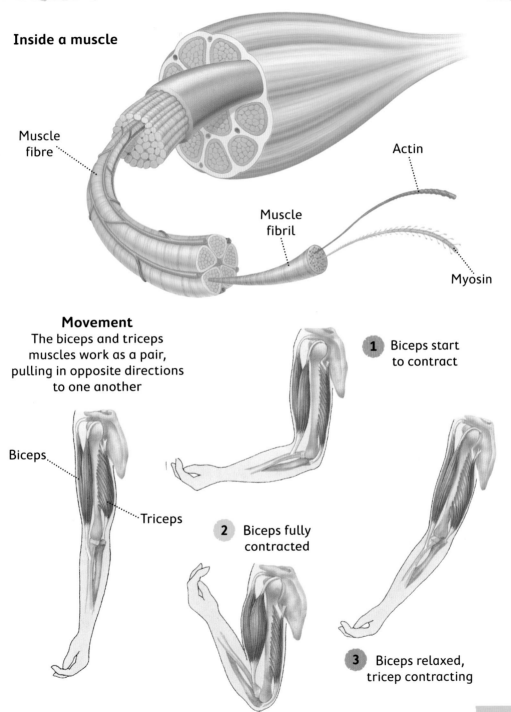

Muscle fibre

Actin

Muscle fibril

Myosin

Movement
The biceps and triceps muscles work as a pair, pulling in opposite directions to one another

Biceps

Triceps

1 Biceps start to contract

2 Biceps fully contracted

3 Biceps relaxed, tricep contracting

Skin, hair and nails

Skin cross-section
Your body is protected
by your skin

Key

1 Keratin layer

2 Gland making oily sebum
to waterproof hair

3 Dermis

4 Hair erector muscle

5 Sweat gland

6 Basal layer, where
new cells grow

7 Epidermis

8 Hair follicle (root)

9 Hair

Hair colour

Different amounts of pigments (coloured substances) called melanin and carotene cause different hair colours

Black curly hair

Blonde wavy hair

Straight red hair

Straight black hair

Inside the finger

Nails protect the ends of your fingers (and toes)

Nail

Key

1. Nail bed
2. Cuticle (skin edge)
3. Nail root
4. Bone

Brain

Controls your actions and responses, as well as allowing
you to think, learn, understand and create

Brain functions
Different areas of the brain's outer
layer deal with messages to and
from certain parts of the body

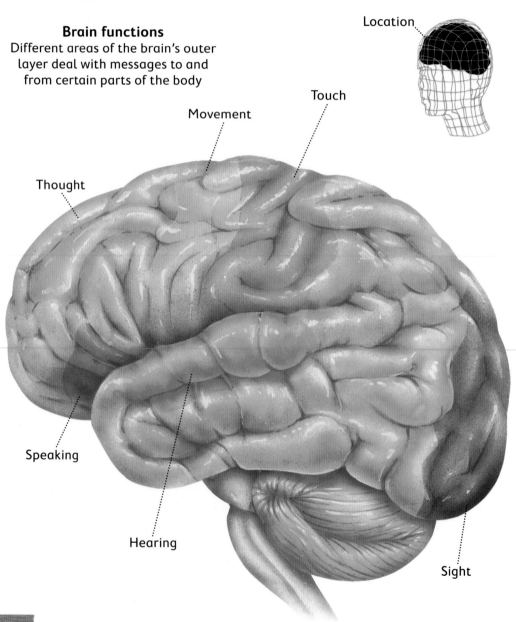

Location

Touch

Movement

Thought

Speaking

Hearing

Sight

Inside the brain

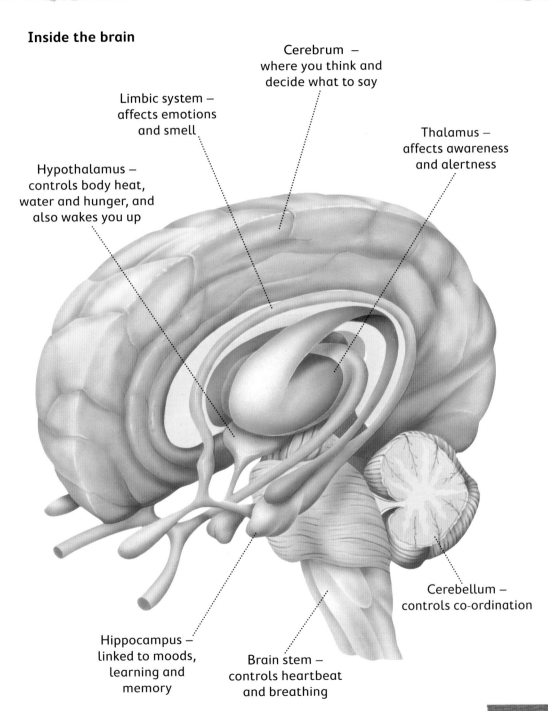

Cerebrum –
where you think and
decide what to say

Limbic system –
affects emotions
and smell

Thalamus –
affects awareness
and alertness

Hypothalamus –
controls body heat,
water and hunger, and
also wakes you up

Cerebellum –
controls co-ordination

Hippocampus –
linked to moods,
learning and
memory

Brain stem –
controls heartbeat
and breathing

Sight

Your body finds out about the world around it by its senses, and your main sense is eyesight

Location

Inside the eye

Eye muscles
that turn
the eye

Tear gland

Iris

Pupil

Tear duct to nose

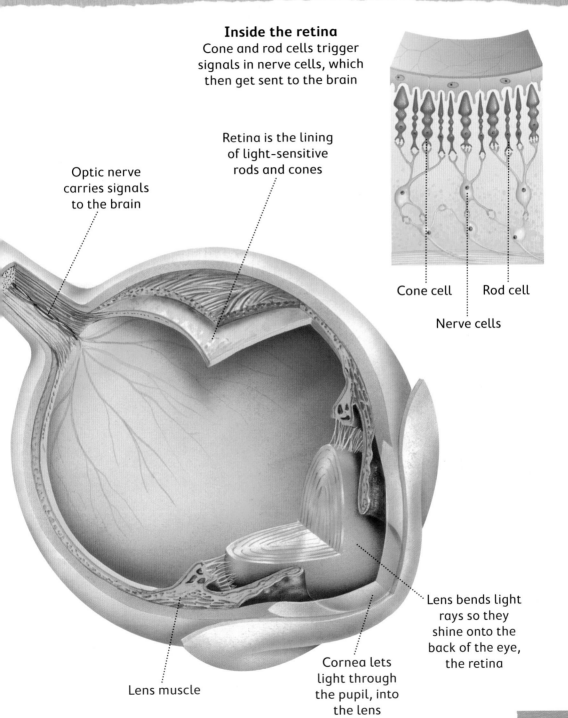

Inside the retina
Cone and rod cells trigger signals in nerve cells, which then get sent to the brain

Retina is the lining of light-sensitive rods and cones

Optic nerve carries signals to the brain

Cone cell

Rod cell

Nerve cells

Lens bends light rays so they shine onto the back of the eye, the retina

Lens muscle

Cornea lets light through the pupil, into the lens

Hearing and speaking

Ears allow you to hear and you use
your vocal cords to speak

How loud?

Volume is measured
in decibels (dB)

Whisper 20 dB

Ordinary speech 60 dB

Loud appliance 75 dB

Motorcycle 100 dB

Jet engine 130 dB

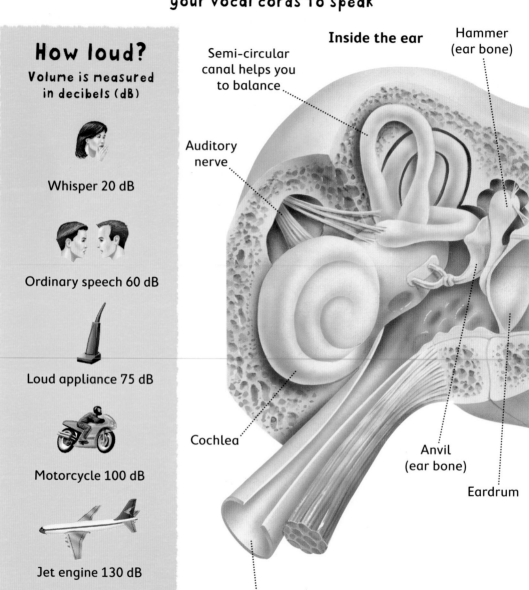

Inside the ear

Hammer
(ear bone)

Semi-circular
canal helps you
to balance

Auditory
nerve

Cochlea

Anvil
(ear bone)

Eardrum

Air tube
to throat

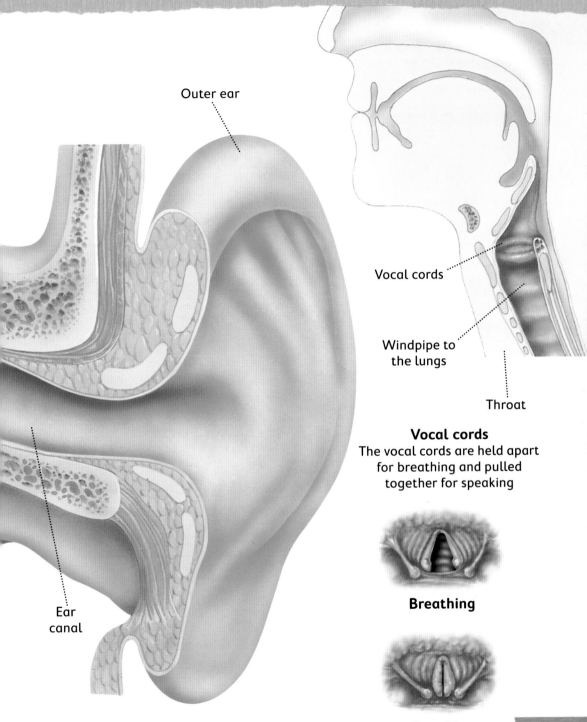

Outer ear

Vocal cords

Windpipe to
the lungs

Throat

Vocal cords
The vocal cords are held apart
for breathing and pulled
together for speaking

Breathing

Ear
canal

Speaking

Taste

The tongue is a flexible muscle used to detect flavour

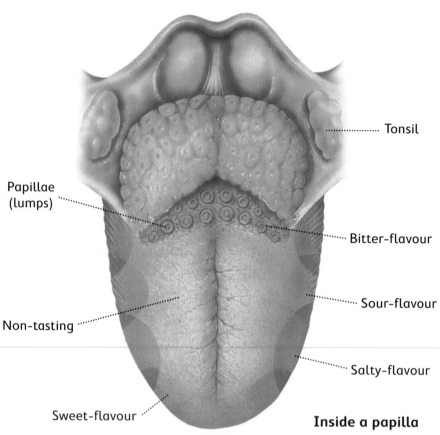

Tonsil

Papillae
(lumps)

Bitter-flavour

Sour-flavour

Non-tasting

Salty-flavour

Sweet-flavour

Inside a papilla

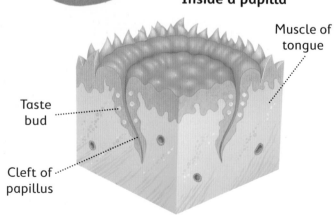

Tongue
Taste buds on the
tongue allow us to taste,
and different areas
sense different flavours.
The tongue can also feel
the texture and
temperature of food

Muscle of
tongue

Taste
bud

Cleft of
papillus

Smell

You cannot see smells (tiny particles floating in the air), but your nose can detect them

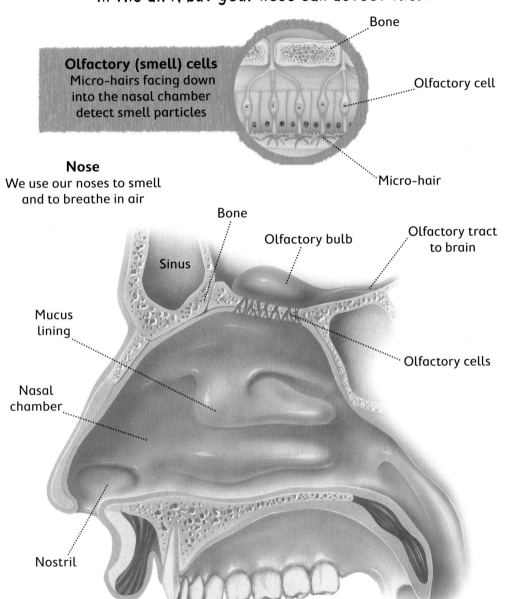

Olfactory (smell) cells
Micro-hairs facing down
into the nasal chamber
detect smell particles

Bone

Olfactory cell

Micro-hair

Nose
We use our noses to smell
and to breathe in air

Bone

Sinus

Olfactory bulb

Olfactory tract
to brain

Mucus
lining

Olfactory cells

Nasal
chamber

Nostril

351

Nervous system

The body's control and communication system, made up of nerves and the brain

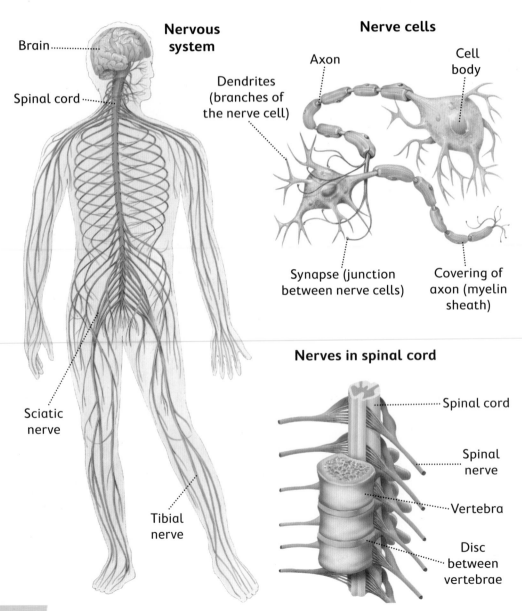

Nervous system

Brain

Spinal cord

Sciatic nerve

Tibial nerve

Nerve cells

Axon

Cell body

Dendrites (branches of the nerve cell)

Synapse (junction between nerve cells)

Covering of axon (myelin sheath)

Nerves in spinal cord

Spinal cord

Spinal nerve

Vertebra

Disc between vertebrae

Immune System

The system of defences that your body uses to prevent or fight off germs

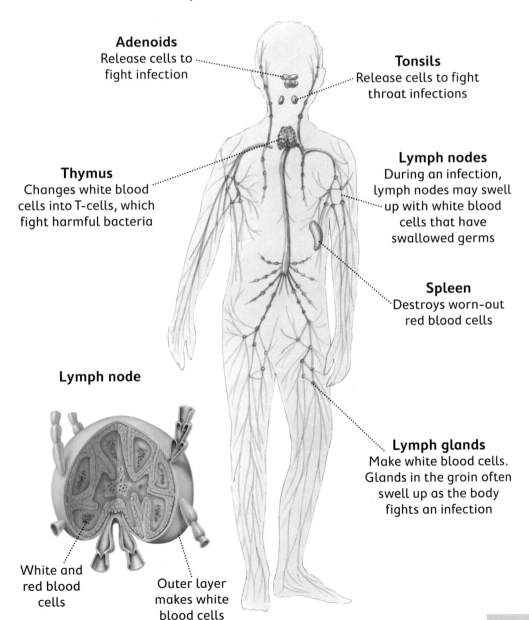

Adenoids
Release cells to fight infection

Tonsils
Release cells to fight throat infections

Thymus
Changes white blood cells into T-cells, which fight harmful bacteria

Lymph nodes
During an infection, lymph nodes may swell up with white blood cells that have swallowed germs

Spleen
Destroys worn-out red blood cells

Lymph node

Lymph glands
Make white blood cells. Glands in the groin often swell up as the body fights an infection

White and red blood cells

Outer layer makes white blood cells

Motorbike
This lightweight, two-wheeled speed machine can reach high speeds and travel long distances

TRANSPORT

Cars

Most cars have four wheels, an engine at the front,
a storage compartment (boot) at the back,
two front seats and two or three rear seats

Early cars

Modern cars have changed greatly in speed and design
since they first appeared over 100 years ago

Benz carriage
Developed by
Karl Benz

Model T Ford
Developed by
Henry Ford

Lanchester
Developed by
Frederick Lanchester

Saloon car
Aston Martin

Windscreen

Roof

Windows

Wing
mirror

Engine-
burns fuel to
power the car

Radiator
grills

Spokes

Wheel

Windscreen
wipers

Tyre

Speed machines
People race cars in competitions around the world. One of the popular races is Formula One (F1)

F1 racing car
These cars are brilliant at speeding round a twisty racetrack

Powerful engine

Rally car
A special version of a normal production car with a tuned-up engine and stronger mechanical parts

Dragster
Used in dragster races – the fastest, loudest form of motor racing

Computer-controlled gearbox

Super sports car
The Bugatti Veyron is the fastest production car in the world

357

Bicycles

Modern bicycles still have the same basic design as old ones. People ride them for fun and exercise

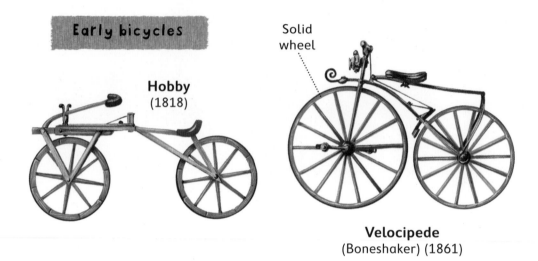

Early bicycles

Hobby
(1818)

Solid
wheel

Velocipede
(Boneshaker) (1861)

Penny Farthing
(early 1870s)

Large front
wheel

High-up
saddle

Small rear
wheel

Pedals
attached to
wheels

Modern bicycles

Seat

Spoke

Handlebars

Crossbar

Mountain bike

Brake cable

Knobbly,
high-grip tyres

Brake pad

Pedal

Drive chain

Tandem
bicycle

Aerodynamic
bicycle

Road race
bicycle

Handlebars are
dropped down

Motorbikes

Like cars, motorbikes have been around for over
100 years. Superbikes are very lightweight and fast

Early motorbikes

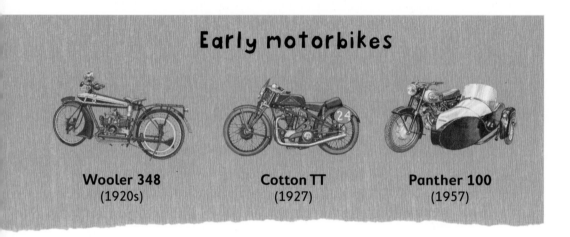

Wooler 348
(1920s)

Cotton TT
(1927)

Panther 100
(1957)

Honda CBR

Windscreen

Brake
disc

Exhaust
pipe

Water-cooled
engine

Lightweight
alloy wheels

Tyres

Yamaha R1

Handlebars

Low-profile seat

Lights

Spokes

Engine

Harley Davidson
Touring motorbike

Throttle

Fuel tank

Forks

'Bucket' seat

Mudguard

Exhaust pipes

Engine

Brake disc

Working machines

Machines are used for all sorts of different jobs, such as tractors that can pull or push farm equipment, and diggers that move earth and dig holes

Trailer

City bus

Articulated truck

Fire tender

Emergency horns

Earth scraper

Blade

Forklift tractor

Backhoe loader

Bulldozer

Teeth

Load

Crane

Concrete mix

Concrete truck

Trains

Since the invention of the first steam engine over **200** years ago, trains are still a popular way to travel

Containers

Freight train
Carries goods such as coal and oil, and materials such as steel and timber

Doors open automatically at stations

London underground
Many cities have underground railways

Maglev train
Uses magnets to glide along tracks

The Flying Scotsman
This train has carried passengers for over 80 years

The driver sits in the cab

Funicular
This train can travel easily up and down steep slopes

Big windows

Bullet train
The fastest wheeled passenger train in the world

Pendolino
Can tilt to travel quickly around corners

Ancient ships

Long before cars and aircraft, people transported valuable
cargoes by boat, while explorers sailed ships across oceans
to discover new lands

Coracle
An early Welsh boat, made
by stretching animal skins
over a wooden frame

Ancient Greek
cargo ship
Ships such as these
could only travel
downwind (in the
direction the wind
is blowing)

Egyptian warship
Early ships such as these were
quite simple, but later they
were made bigger and
included up to 50 oars

Viking longship
These light ships could
sail up shallow rivers,
but were also good
enough to sail in the
open ocean

When the wind
was still, rowers
powered the
boat

Flat-bottomed pirate ship
Being flat-bottomed meant the ship was very fast

Square, bamboo sails

Three masts

Chinese junk
Chinese pirates sailed in ships called junks. These were often captured trading vessels

Boats made of cedar wood and reeds

Phoenician ship
About 2000 years ago, the Phoenician people sailed on long journeys using the stars to navigate (find their way)

Water transport

Throughout history, ships have been used in battles.
Today, ships and boats are also used for fun, and people
even go on ships for holidays

Hydrofoil
These watercraft 'fly'
above the surface on
wing-like foils

Foils

Oil supertanker
Transports oil
around the world

Long hull
(main body)

Aircraft landing

Aircraft carrier
Floating air bases designed
to go anywhere for war

Pool

Cruise liner
Luxury hotels on
the ocean

Passenger hovercraft
Can 'fly' off the water onto a
ramp to load and unload

Skirt

Main sail

Yacht
Mainly small, light sailing
craft. This exploded view
shows how the different
parts fit together

Racing catamaran
A boat with two hulls

Deck

Keel — used for control
and stability while sailing

Submarines and submersibles

Submarines are normally used for warfare and submersibles for exploration

Russian Typhoon
The biggest and fastest subs were built in the 1970s and 1980s

Living quarters

Propeller turned by hand

Torpedo firing room

Turtle
The first combat submarine made its first test drive in 1776

TRIESTE

Trieste
The two person submarine successfully ventured to the Mariana Trench – the deepest part of any ocean

Two-person crew sat in this sphere, which measured 2.1 metres across

Periscope
(vertical telescope)

Rudder (angles to
steer left or right)

Engine
room

ROV Jason
This submersible was
launched in 1988 and lets
explorers investigate
wrecks from sea level

Manipulator
arm to collect
samples

Tray for
collecting
samples from
the seabed

Polaris submarine
The Royal Navy had
four of these nuclear
missile boats

Aircraft

People first tried to fly hundreds of years ago.
Over 200 years ago in France, the Montgolfier brothers
made a large balloon and were the first people to fly

Hot-air balloon
Balloons do not
really fly — they float

Hang-glider
A glider is an aircraft
without an engine

Early aircraft

Fabric-covered
wings

1903 Wright Flyer
The Wright Brothers
completed the first-ever
flight in a controlled
aircraft

Spirit of St Louis
In 1927, Charles Lindbergh
completed the first non-
stop flight over the Atlantic
in this aeroplane

Modern aircraft

Concorde
The first supersonic (faster than the speed of sound) airliner in the world

Airbus A380
The world's largest passenger plane first flew in 2005. It is also known as a 'double-decker'

Very long wings

Sailplane
This glider is so light and streamlined that it loses height very slowly as it glides

Chinook helicopter
Used by air forces and civilians in more than 20 countries worldwide

Rotor blades provide lift

373

War planes

During times of war, planes attack the enemy,
drop bombs and carry troops and equipment

Sopwith Camel
One of the best fighter
planes of World War I
(1914–1918)

Biplanes such as this have
two sets of main wings,
one above the other

Supermarine Spitfire
First flew in 1936 and is
one of the world's most
famous aircraft

Fuel tank

German Junkers 87
dive-bomber
One of the most feared
aircraft in World War II
(1939–1945)

Propeller

374

Bomb explosion

German Messerschmitt 262
Flew in 1944 and carried out bombing raids, but its heavy bombs slowed it down

F-35B
Lightning fighter-bomber
First roared into the skies in 2006, and is one of the world's most advanced aircraft

Radar

Cockpit

Turbojet engine

B-2 Spirit
A long-distance bomber and spyplane

INDEX